Tnotn21

D0193813

Locke

on Government

This is an excellent philosophical introduction to the study of Locke's *Second Treatise* . . . There is no work in print that is comparable in terms of its combination of a genuinely philosophical approach to the text, accessibility to beginners and its concentration exclusively on Locke's moral and political philosophy. It will make a very valuable companion text for undergraduate courses that examine the *Second Treatise* and equally valuable text for more advanced courses that begin with an overview of the most important issues in the book.

A. John Simmons, *University of Virginia*

Written specifically for students coming to Locke for the first time, *Locke on Government* is an invaluable guide to his political thought. Much of what has been written on the *Second Treatise of Government* in the last few decades has taken a 'history of ideas' approach; this book focuses on the philosophical aspects of Locke's work.

The *Second Treatise* is seen as a defence of violent revolution against Charles II and James II, and D. A. Lloyd Thomas gives special attention to Locke's radical position. In addition, he considers other fundamental issues of the *Second Treatise*, such as Locke's attempt to show how legitimate political authority can be based on consent and his defence of a natural right to private property.

Written with the student in mind, *Locke on Government* will make an excellent introduction to one of the most important figures in political thought.

D. A. Lloyd Thomas is Senior Lecturer in Philosophy at King's College London. He is the author of *In Defence of Liberalism* (1988).

**Routledge
Philosophy
GuideBooks**

Edited by Tim Crane and Jonathan Wolff
University College London

Locke on Human Understanding
E. J. Lowe

Plato and the *Republic*
Nickolas Pappas

Forthcoming:
Heidegger's *Being and Time*
Stephen Mulhall

LONDON AND NEW YORK

outledge Philosophy GuideBook to

Locke
on Government

■ D. A. Lloyd Thomas

ROUTLEDGE

First published 1995
by Routledge
11 New Fetter Lane,
London EC4P 4EE

Simultaneously published in the
USA and Canada
by Routledge
29 West 35th Street
New York NY 10001

© 1995 D. A. Lloyd Thomas

Text design: Barker/Hilsdon

Typeset in Times and Frutiger by
Florencetype Ltd, Stoodleigh,
Devon

Printed and bound in Great Britain
by TJ Press Ltd, Padstow, Cornwall

*British Library Cataloguing in
Publication Data*
A catalogue record for this book is
available from the British Library.

*Library of Congress Cataloging in
Publication Data*
Locke on government/David Lloyd
Thomas.
p. cm. – (Routledge Philosophy
GuideBooks)
Includes bibliographical references
and index.
1. Locke, John, 1632–1704. Essay
concerning the true original extent
and end of civil government.
I. Title. II. Series.
JC153.L87L58 1995
320.5′ 12′ 092–dc20   95–5514
                                    CIP

ISBN 0–415–09534–4 (hbk)
ISBN 0–415–09533–6 (pbk)

For Doris and Barbara,
Katie and Sally

Contents

Preface

This book is intended to be of particular use to students of the history of political theory in departments of government, political science and philosophy. It introduces John Locke's *Second Treatise of Government* from a serious philosophical point of view to undergraduates and beginning postgraduates. It is hoped that it may be of interest to their teachers also. Efforts have been made to produce a text intelligible to someone reading Locke for the first time, including the interested general reader. Much of the very great deal written on the *Second Treatise* in the last few decades, though both good and influential, has taken an 'historical' or 'history of ideas' approach. The closest to my own philosophical style of approach is to be found in A. John Simmons' two excellent recent studies of Locke, *The Lockean Theory of Rights* (1992) and *On the Edge of Anarchy* (1993). The present work is much shorter and simpler, however; and, as is only to be expected, the interpretations offered here are different on many points.

Scholars of Locke's political writings disagree about what his position was on many issues. This is not usually because Locke was obscure, or because he contradicted himself. The *Second Treatise* was intended to be a work of political persuasion, not an academic text. Sometimes Locke left his position on contentious issues open to more than one interpretation in order to avoid alienating possible allies. The interpretations put forward here are believed to be reasonable and supported by the text. However, it cannot be pretended that they are always universally accepted as the correct interpretation of Locke. I could have attempted to develop cases for my own interpretations of Locke against alternatives more frequently, but to have done this in all cases would have made the book several times its present length. For the same reason I have avoided surveys of the literature indicating what interpretations besides my own are available. The book has been written with a consciousness that students, in particular, often do not have the time for leisurely reading, and are seeking to learn as much as possible in the limited time they have available.

The series of which this book is a part has been designed as a set of companions to famous books in philosophy rather than to famous philosophers. Attention is given here almost entirely to the *Second Treatise*, with a little supplementation from the *First Treatise*. To my knowledge the views attributed to Locke in the *Second Treatise* remain plausible when account is taken of his other writings. However, no attempt will be made to demonstrate in detail that this is so. The *Two Treatises of Government* stand fairly much on their own in Locke's writings; separate even from his works on toleration. Locke's desire to conceal his authorship of the *Two Treatises* prevented him from making allusions to other works of his, the authorship of which he had acknowledged. A fruitful attempt to trace connections between the *Two Treatises* and Locke's *Essay Concerning Human Understanding* is to be found in Chapter 1 of Ruth Grant's *John Locke's Liberalism* (1987).

References to Locke's *Two Treatises of Government* are given by I or II followed by the section number. Thus II.27 indicates the *Second Treatise*, section 27. When quotations are given from the *Second Treatise*, the version of the text followed is as printed in *John Locke: Political Writings*, edited with an introduction by David Wootton (Harmondsworth: Penguin, 1993). All other references are given in the style of the Harvard system. Only author, date of publication and page number are given in the text. Full details of the work cited are given in the bibliography. Thus 'Simmons 1993, 73' indicates A. John Simmons, *On the Edge of Anarchy*, p. 73.

My very great thanks go to Jo Wolff, joint editor of this series. He has read all of the text at least once, and in many cases more than once. He has made innumerable careful, helpful and improving suggestions, only a few of which are specifically acknowledged in the text. There are many, many more places where he has rescued me from myself that have only this as their acknowledgement. He originally suggested that I write this contribution to the series. Throughout the whole time during which I have been supplying him with material he has dealt with it patiently and industriously, and has gently encouraged me to emulate the Puritan Work Ethic a little more after the example set by my author.

I also owe much to Jerry Cohen, not only for his detailed criticism of an earlier draft of the chapter on rebellion, but also for the great encouragement he gave to me to develop that piece. My debt to him is much wider than that: he has clarified my ideas on other aspects of Locke, especially on property, and on many other questions in political philosophy. His work is a model of what I would like to be able to do.

The revision of the text has been very much assisted by Routledge's readers. The identity of one, A. John Simmons, has been revealed to me, but not that of the other. To both of these people I am very grateful for their detailed, careful and profitable suggestions, and for their encouragement of the project as whole. If time had allowed I would have followed their suggestions for changes in even more places than I have been able to.

My ideas have benefited from – indeed often have come to exist because of – discussion of material with students and colleagues at many lectures, seminars and tutorials in the University of London. It should be said more often how fortunate we who teach at that institution are in having so many excellent students. Much benefit also has been derived from discussions with colleagues at various seminars in the University of London, particularly those organized by Jo Wolff and Bill Hart; and also a seminar at the University of Oxford organized by John Gray and Alan Ryan. John Milton has introduced me to the intricacies of real Locke scholarship. To my Department and to King's College, London I am very grateful for sabbatical terms which provided much of the time for getting this finished.

My greatest debt is to Anne Lloyd Thomas, who has helped in more ways than anyone else, and in more ways than I am able to think of at once.

In writing on an author as prominent as Locke, completion is more a matter of decision than of having come to the natural end of a task. There is always more of what has been written on Locke that could have been considered. My hope is that although, inevitably, this book is much less complete than it could have been, it will prove to be reasonably reliable in indicating the main structure of Locke's political theory. It is a theory that deserves our respect: it has had more influence than any other work in Western political theory on how the contemporary world actually is today.

Chapter 1

Introduction

The context of the writing of the *Second Treatise*

Locke's *Second Treatise of Government* was written a little over three hundred years ago, in an immensely different world from that in which we read it. This prompts questions about how we should approach the text; questions we do not face when reading contemporary political philosophy. The answers fall into two groups, the historical and the philosophical. The former says that we should take seriously the fact that the *Second Treatise* is located in a very different world from our own, politically and intellectually. We should try to understand how the ideas and arguments of the *Second Treatise* were related to that world, in particular to the political situation of Locke's time. We should not assume that the concepts and arguments to be found in the book have any, or at any rate any

straightforward, relationship to our political concerns. Our intellectual assumptions are not Locke's, and our political concerns are not his either. The *Second Treatise* is not to be read as if it were a contribution to a contemporary journal of political philosophy.

This approach is commonest amongst historians of ideas such as Richard Ashcraft (Ashcraft 1986) and John Dunn (Dunn 1969). By contrast, the philosophical approach, as represented, for example, by A. John Simmons (Simmons 1992 and 1993), invites us to lift Locke's text out of its context of three hundred years ago, and to examine its arguments on topics that continue to be of interest to contemporary political philosophy: the grounds of political obligation, democracy, the limits of the powers of government and the circumstances in which revolution is morally acceptable. As one with a philosophical background I incline towards the latter approach, but not without qualification: Locke's writings did address the particular political issues of his day; issues which, at least in that form, are no longer with us. Even so, there are sufficient general similarities between the political issues he thought about, and the issues which concern us now, for his ideas and arguments to remain relevant to us. This, indeed, is why the continued study of the *Second Treatise* in courses on political theory and political philosophy remains appropriate, and why Locke's political writings are not only of concern to students of English political ideas in the late seventeenth century.

The primary concern in what follows will be with whether the positions Locke is putting forward are true, or rationally defensible. Locke's arguments will be taken seriously as arguments: it will be of concern whether they really do follow. It is intended to take the text of the *Second Treatise* in the spirit in which it was offered; that is, as giving reasons why we should believe certain things about what we ought to do in the political sphere. The text will not be taken as merely an instance of a certain type of political 'ideology', stuck for all time in the mud of a particular historical context.

But this is not to deny that we can learn much of relevance from some awareness of the political situation in which Locke was writing. From time to time I will comment on how his theory connects up with the political situation of his time. Indeed, knowledge of the circumstances in which the *Second Treatise* was written tends to confirm my interpretation of the text itself: that it is primarily (if not always overtly) out to show that it can be morally justifiable for a people to embark upon all-out armed rebellion against those who claim to be their government.

A few remarks therefore are appropriate about the historical setting in which the *Two Treatises* were written. They were published in 1689, just after the 'Glorious Revolution' had replaced James II with William and Mary. They were probably written, however, in the early 1680s in the household of the Earl of Shaftesbury, to whom Locke was then a kind of private secretary and personal 'think-tank'. Earlier Shaftesbury had been a leading member of the government of Charles II, but by the early 1680s he had fallen out with the King over his policies towards Catholics, towards France and particularly over his distaste for Parliament and his absolutist tendencies.

The impression that the *Two Treatises* were composed after the revolution is given by a few passages that prove to have been inserted just before publication. One such is the Preface, where King William is referred to as 'our Great Restorer', and where Locke remarks on the fact that the latter part of the *First Treatise* (a refutation of the monarchist views of Sir Robert Filmer) is missing. It is odd that Locke should have given the manuscript of the *First Treatise* to the publisher in a state where it breaks off abruptly in mid-sentence. Perhaps Locke thought it urgent to get the *Two Treatises* published, and their appearance did indeed suit the hour. Another apparent addition of 1689 is section 222 of the *Second Treatise*, which contains a direct reference to the policies James II was pursuing just before he was overthrown.

By the early 1680s Shaftesbury was a leading figure amongst the opposition Whigs. They attempted to get a bill through Parliament (an Exclusion Bill) to prevent the then Duke of York (later James II), a Catholic, from succeeding to the throne. These attempts failed. Charles II dissolved Parliament and Shaftesbury's thoughts turned from Parliamentary opposition to outright rebellion. Locke's task was to provide a defence of radical Whig policy which would appeal to educated, well-to-do Whigs, doubtful of going so far as outright revolution. In the event Locke had to go into exile in Holland in 1683 for reasons of personal safety, and the *Two Treatises* did not become public until 1689. So instead of persuading people to start a revolution, as Locke had intended, the *Second Treatise* ended up by providing an *ex post facto* justification of the revolution of 1688.

At present there is some reluctance, both on the left and on the right, to accept that the most influential political philosopher to have written in English was, in his theories and in practice, a committed revolutionary for something like a decade of his life. For Marxists and the left this may be because of difficulty in reconciling Locke's apparent defence of the propertied, and his bourgeois image, with his being a true revolutionary. However, he was much more of a revolutionary than most Western left-wing intellectuals of the last few decades. For the right this reluctance may be because of a desire to perceive British political history as an incremental and evolutionary process, and a lack of willingness to view the settlement of 1689 as indeed the outcome of a revolution.

Locke's life

Locke was born in 1632, and brought up near Pensford, in Somerset, not far south of Bristol. His family had Puritan leanings and Parliamentary sympathies during the Civil War. They lived in modest but comfortable circumstances. In later life Locke had sufficient income from family estates to live the life of a gentleman of modest means. He went to Westminster School in 1647, during the Civil War, and continued on to Christ Church, Oxford in 1652. He had his reservations about the intellectual atmosphere of Oxford at the time, especially its pedantry. Indeed his relations with Oxford were often uneasy. Even in the last years of his life a meeting of heads of Oxford colleges resolved that tutors should be instructed not to discuss Locke's *Essay Concerning Human Understanding* with their students (Cranston 1957, 468). Nevertheless, Locke stayed on at Oxford after his graduation in 1656, and retained his connection with Christ Church until 1684, when he was ejected from his place at the insistence of Charles II. After graduation Locke cultivated an interest in medicine, and became a friend of the great chemist Robert Boyle. Locke qualified for his M.A. in 1658, was Lecturer in Greek in 1661 and 1662, Lecturer in Rhetoric for 1663, and Censor of Moral Philosophy for 1664 (Milton 1994, 32).

Locke's first works were written at Oxford: the *Two Tracts on Government* (Locke 1967) between 1660 and 1662, and the *Essays on the Law of Nature* (Locke 1954), probably a course of lectures to begin with, in 1663–4. These works were not published during Locke's lifetime. They were not in keeping with his later 'liberalism'. The *Two Tracts* argued against religious toleration. The *Essays on the Law of Nature* denied that legitimate government rested upon the consent of the people.

Locke briefly tried the diplomatic life as a member of a mission to Cleves in the winter of 1665–6, and with sufficient success for another post to be offered. But much the most important development for his political interests was his joining the London household of Anthony Ashley Cooper (in due course first Earl of Shaftesbury) in 1667. Shaftesbury was a leading Whig grandee at the time, with whom Locke became a very close friend and associate. The relationship was confirmed early when Locke made use of his medical knowledge to direct an operation on Shaftesbury which (miraculously) saved his life. Their association mostly depended, however, on their pursuit of common political objectives.

Living in Shaftesbury's household brought Locke into the centre of English political life and, as Shaftesbury became more resolutely opposed to the policies of Charles II, it involved Locke in the dangers and uncertainties of his patron's own situation. In the views of both Ashcraft (Ashcraft 1986, 121) and Laslett (Locke 1988, 29), Locke was suspected of being the author of *A Letter from a Person of Quality to his Friend in the Country*. This pamphlet infuriated the government, and may have led to Locke's hasty departure for France in 1675.[1] Locke travelled widely there, spending most of his time in Montpellier and Paris. He met several leading intellectuals of his day. By the time he returned from France in 1679 Locke may have made substantial progress with early drafts of the *Essay Concerning Human Understanding*.

Locke's 'liberalism' arose out of his association with Shaftesbury. *An Essay Concerning Toleration* (1667) (Locke 1993) and the *Two Treatises of Government* were probably written in Shaftesbury's household, and quite possibly in response to his

5

requests. Ashcraft dates the composition of the *Two Treatises* at about 1680–2, and Laslett has them started a little earlier, in 1679.

In 1683, following the discovery of the Rye House plot on the life of Charles II (in which Locke may have been implicated) he had to go into exile again, this time to Holland. Locke had probably completed the *Two Treatises* by this time, and wished to avoid the fate of Algernon Sydney, who had been executed for writing a treasonable manuscript. Shaftesbury died in 1683. Locke lived in Holland with many other English refugees from the oppression of Charles II and James II until returning to England in 1689, after the success of the Glorious Revolution. In that year Locke also published (also anonomously) the *Epistola de Tolerantia*, probably written in Amsterdam in 1685 (Horton and Mendus 1991, 5). An English translation of this, made by William Popple, also appeared in that year under the title *A Letter Concerning Toleration* (see Horton and Mendus 1991, or Locke 1993). The only publication of that memorable year Locke acknowledged was the *Essay Concerning Human Understanding*, probably completed by the end of 1686 (Cranston 1957, 208). Locke was angry when he discovered that his Dutch friend Limborch had disclosed his authorship of the *Epistola de Tolerantia* (Cranston 1957, 332). He never publically acknowledged his authorship of the *Two Treatises* during his lifetime, despite the fact that many knew of it.

It is hard to say why Locke was so secretive. We must remember, though, that the *Two Treatises* were written in a far from tolerant political environment, and that Sydney's execution had been for views no more radical than Locke's. In the 1670s and 1680s, under Charles II and James II, some of the methods of the modern police state had already been deployed: spies, informers, the manipulation of juries to gain convictions and the kidnapping of political exiles. It was dangerous to argue for the right of the people to resist established government, with force if necessary. We study the *Second Treatise* in liberal societies and in an academic context, but these were not the circumstances in which it was composed. These are reasons why Locke may have been reluctant to acknowledge authorship of the *Two Treatises*. It is true that Locke's side had won by 1689, but Locke could not know when he published that the settlement would last. On the other hand, he must have wished to make a contribution to helping it last. It is also true, however, that Locke did not acknowledge authorship of other much less controversial works, so it may be that he was just inclined to be secretive. He lived in times when it was not wise to be too open. In the text of the *Second Treatise*, as we shall see, Locke was also occasionally less than completely frank about the views that are in fact to be found in it. This is partly due to its being intended to be politically persuasive, and the wish to avoid alienating potential allies.

Locke spent much of the remainder of his life in the household of Sir Francis and Lady Masham in the countryside not far north of London. Locke had had a close relationship with Lady Masham before her marriage. She was Damaris Cudworth, daughter of the Cambridge Platonist Ralph Cudworth. Locke was not inactive in the later years of his life, and made frequent visits to London. He had a prominent role in the political life of the country now that he was on the 'right' side. He was Commissioner for Appeals, and a Commissioner for Trade, a very responsible position dealing mostly with the problems of the English colonies. He influenced the repeal of the Act for the Regulation of Printing in 1695 and also the re-coinage of the debased English currency in the 1690s. Before his death in 1704 Locke was not only an internationally renowned intellectual figure, but also moved in the most influential political circles in England. Apart from further editions of the *Essay*, Locke published a number of minor works in his later years. *Some Considerations on the Lowering of Interest and Raising the Value of Money* appeared in 1691, though it had been written in 1668 (Cranston 1957, 117). The *Second Letter for Toleration* (1691) and the *Third Letter for Toleration* (1692) were responses to criticisms of *A Letter Concerning Toleration* made by Jonas Proast. *Some Thoughts on Education* followed in 1693, and *The Reasonableness of Christianity* in 1695.

Locke's character

What kind of a man was Locke? This is not an easy question to answer, for in the space of 300 years even the categories in which we assess character change. We know, from the elderly of our acquaintance, or, if we are old enough, from our own recollections, how certain types of attitude and traits of character once common disappear in later generations. Some of the external circumstances of Locke's life are easier to reconstruct. Locke never seems to have lacked friends, but in most periods of his life he was rootless. In no place did he live very long continuously, and often he lived between two places, for example, between London and Oxford in the Shaftesbury days, and between the Mashams' house and London in his later years. He travelled frequently, not only when abroad, but also in England. He settled down with no one, had no wife or children, and was always a lodger or guest in someone else's establishment. For much of his life Locke was quite comfortably off. Though he had neither the means nor the desire to live lavishly, his life was not circumscribed by lack of money, and he died quite well off. By the standards of modern academic life he enjoyed considerable leisure. For long periods his time was largely free for travel, reading, discussion, reflection and writing.

The most relevant aspect of Locke's character for us is revealed in his writings – a powerful, curious, original and well-informed intellect, motivated by considerable intellectual energy. His intellect, wit and learning recommended him to the distinguished minds of his day, including Boyle, Newton and Wren. His intellect was perhaps of more generous proportions than his character generally. Detachment from the real world, and lack of commitment, so often the fault of the philosophical intellect, were not amongst Locke's vices. But his mind seems to have had a certain matter-of-factness about it, characteristic of Anglo-Saxon empiricism, which left him largely unaware of the aesthetic aspects of things. He was profoundly religious, very much a Protestant, and very prejudiced against Catholics. A tendency towards puritanism often goes with philistinism, but in Locke it did not go with an excessive suspicion of pleasure. He was very preoccupied with money and tended to be parsimonious. He was capable of being quite short and ill-tempered with his friends. But he also sustained a number of friendships over long periods of his life, and could show striking loyalty, for example, to Shaftesbury. He could be careful and crafty in his dealings (and in his writings) to the point of deviousness. He was very preoccupied with his own health. Locke was perhaps one of those people who wish to protect a place private from everyone else. He was jealous of his independence and autonomy, and not only intellectually committed to the doctrine that persons own themselves.

Chapter 2

Social contract and the state

Introduction

In the arts, works once thought to be outrageous innovations sometimes become the ackowledged masterpieces of a later period. So, too, with the principles of political organization. What, for us, are obvious, even platitudinous, political principles were once regarded as radicalism and subversion. Locke's *Second Treatise* is not the first presentation of what are now regarded as some of the most evident of political principles. But it is the most influential. At the time Locke wrote the *Second Treatise* these principles were not universally accepted. It is appropriate that we note them at the beginning. This is not just because it is necessary as an introduction to Locke's argument. Since the triumph of political liberalism in the train of the Eastern European revolutions of the late 1980s, these principles have come to receive the assent of the whole

respectable political world. Even disreputable holders of political power usually avoid their explicit denial, though not, regrettably, their violation.

These are the principles, which are evident to us, but which were radical and unacceptable for many of Locke's contemporaries:

1. The citizens of a state, no matter what differences might exist between them in social status, authority, or wealth, are basically equal in political standing (II.95).
2. Each citizen is equal to all the others in that each possesses certain individual rights which limit what any citizen may do to any other. These rights also limit what the state may do to any of its citizens.
3. Those who hold authority in the system of government, or in other political institutions, are to be regarded as doing so not for their own gain, advantage or prestige, but in order to further the good of their fellow citizens.
4. Government is instituted to ensure that the rights of all citizens are respected, and to promote the good of the citizens.
5. As governments are instituted only for the benefit of the citizens, if the citizens no longer consent to how they are being governed and wish to be rid of their governors, the government ceases to have any moral right to be in power. In these circumstances the use of force by the people, if necessary, is morally justified as a last resort.

It is to be emphasized that although I believe the substance of these five principles to be beyond doubt attributable to Locke, they are not stated anywhere in the *Second Treatise* in the form given here.

One representative of a conservative view in Locke's time was Sir Robert Filmer, whose *Patriarcha* (Filmer 1949) was the object of Locke's attack in his *First Treatise*. Filmer held that from the political point of view (as from any other) citizens were unequal and related to one another by a divinely instituted heirarchy, with the monarchy at its head on earth. Citizens had such rights as the monarch might choose to bestow upon them, and they had no rights independent of what was established by law. The monarch enjoyed his position by divine right, as passed down from the original right of Adam, upon whom God had bestowed the first kingship. The position of the king in no way depended upon the consent of his subjects. The people had no right to oppose or depose their monarch.

Filmer could be described as a defender of the 'deference' society. He held that even before the formation of political society, or even during a period of anarchy, when ordered political life was in abeyance, some people were in a 'natural' relationship of subordination to others. Locke, by contrast, believed in the natural equality of persons. In the Lockean state of nature people stand in a relationship of equality to one another. Only after the construction of political society do people come to hold unequal positions. That inequality is artificial, the result of the deliberate construction of political society. Filmer's attitudes were very common in Locke's time, though they will strike us as quaint now, when only a curious section of the English upper classes believes in deference in this sense. However, a more widespread relative of this view is to be found in some contemporary attitudes of racial superiority.

A conservatism of a very different (and much more intelligent) type was to be found in Thomas Hobbes' *Leviathan*, first published in 1651 (Hobbes 1968). Hobbes had argued that in order to establish a secure peace, rational men, who found themselves in a state of nature, would make a covenant with each other, having the effect of creating a sovereign power. The sovereign's commands would be law, and the sovereign would also have the coercive power (limitless compared to the power of any ordinary citizen) to enforce that law. In order to preserve peace all citizens ought to obey the commands of the sovereign. Hobbes believed that there was no option between virtually unconditional obedience to the commands of the sovereign, and the disintegration of the sovereign power, leading to civil war. The will of the sovereign ought not to be thwarted on the supposed ground that it was in violation of the citizen's natural rights. No limitation on the authority of the sovereign power by the citizens can be allowed. Thus, of the Lockean principles mentioned above, Hobbes certainly could not have accepted (2), (4) or (5).

Locke wished to develop a theory of legitimate political authority which was consistent with the five principles mentioned, and which repudiated reactionaries such as Filmer and authoritarians such as Hobbes. This chapter will outline how Locke constructed such a theory. But Locke did intend it to be a theory of *legitimate government*, and this was where the major problem arose. For Locke's opponents, such as Filmer, had claimed that if government was supposed to rest on the consent of the governed, it would be impossible to show how any legitimate government could exist. I will argue that if it is held that government rests on the consent of the governed to an original compact, then it *does* prove impossible to show that legitimate political authority exists. But in the end this is not so embarrassing for someone defending the five principles. For there is in fact *no* way in which it can be shown that legitimate political authority exists, in my view. (In fact I do not believe that such a thing as legitimate political authority exists, and thus it is no surprise that there is no way in which its existence can be shown.) Thus Locke's failure to show that it exists does not weaken support for the principles. This is consistent with saying that there may be reason to obey (some) governments: indeed that there may be good *moral* reason to obey them. For, as will be explained in more detail later, not all reasons, or even all moral reasons, for obeying governments are reasons for accepting that they have legitimate authority. The argument of this chapter will be that although Locke is unable to establish legitimate political authority on the basis of consent, he is still correct to put forward the five principles.

In his *Second Treatise* Locke wants to show two things about the state. The first is that there can be a legitimate state, i.e. one the existence of which is consistent with its citizens' natural rights. Here Locke stands in opposition to those anarchists who deny that a legitimate state, in this sense, is possible. The other is that armed rebellion, all-out revolution, can be justified when the conditions for the legitimacy of government cease to be satisfied. As has just been explained, Locke is conscious of the conservative objection that if you support the legitimacy of government then you cannot also say that rebellion is sometimes justifiable. He proposes to meet this objection by developing a 'core' social contract theory from which both the possibility of legitimate government, and of justifiable rebellion, can be derived. I will now expound that 'core' theory.

Natural law and natural rights

Locke's account of how a legitimate state is possible depends on his conception of natural law and natural right. Modern political theory does not make use of these terms in the same way as Locke did, so some indication of what he meant by them is appropriate. It might seem that Locke had no coherent conception of the law of nature. It is true that no part of the *Second Treatise* is set aside for a systematic exposition of the ideas of natural law and natural right. Nevertheless, Locke appears to have had a coherent conception of these terms. It may be reconstructed from his frequent, if scattered, references to natural law in the *Second Treatise*, and from his early lectures given at Oxford, and edited and published by von Leyden as *Essays on the Law of Nature* (Locke 1954).

'Natural law' in Locke refers not to scientific laws governing physical processes, but to normative laws. Natural laws in Locke are laws in accordance with which human conduct ought to occur, not laws in accordance with which people always do act. To convey Locke's idea of natural law it is convenient to separate two aspects it has. First, there is what might be called the 'formal' aspect of Locke's conception of natural law. This includes the features of his conception which indicate what is necessary for something to be a law of nature, but without indicating what, in particular, laws of nature require us to do. The second aspect is the particular structure and content Locke thought the law of nature had. In this respect Locke's conception differs from that of other natural law theorists of his time.

Locke's view of the formal aspects of the law of nature is conventional for his time.

1. A law of nature is a law prescribing conduct which is separate from and independent of the conventions of mankind: independent, that is, of the positive laws of states, and of established social conventions or customs. Two ideas are covered by the term 'independent'. The first is that the foundation or justification of natural law does not depend on what the normative conventions of mankind happen to be. It is justified by something lying outside or 'above' the mere conventions of mankind. The other is that positive law or social convention may or may

not correspond in fact to what is required by the law of nature.
(Of course it always *ought* to correspond if you are a natural
law theorist.)

2. The law of nature is the law of reason. In acting in accordance
   with the law of nature people act in accordance with reason: in
   acting contrary to it they act against reason. We can come to
   know what the law of nature requires of us by making use of
   our reason.

3. The law of nature is the law God requires us to act in accordance with. We can know what the law of nature requires of us
   by consulting the will of God as revealed in scripture. Locke
   assumes that the results of our attempts to find out through
   reason what the law of nature requires will be consistent with
   the results of our attempts to find out what it requires by reve-
   lation. The true will of God could not be contrary to reason.

4. The law of nature is universal. It applies to all persons at all
   times and in all places. All persons ought to be treated in accordance with the law of nature. All persons (who have reached
   the age of reason) ought to treat others in accordance with the
   law of nature. The laws of all states, and the social conventions
   and customs of all communities ought to be consistent with the
   law of nature. Even so, the law of nature allows for possible
   variation in the positive laws of different countries, and for vari-
   ations in social conventions and customs. It does not precisely
   determine all norms of human conduct.

The characterization of the law of nature just given does not tell us
what the law of nature requires: it does not tell us what, in fact, the
law of nature wants us to do. Nor does it say *how* it is supposed to
be justified by reason. We shall now see what Locke thinks is involved
in applying reason to discover what the law of nature is. First Locke
postulates a 'fundamental law of nature': 'The fundamental law of
nature being that all, as much as may be, should be preserved'(II.183.
See also II.16, II.134 and II.149). What Locke means by saying that
a particular (non-fundamental, or derivative) law of nature is required
by reason is that the derivative law of nature can be rationally justified
on the basis of the fundamental law of nature. What does 'rationally

justified' mean in this context? It means that the derivative law of nature can be shown to be rationally necessary, given the fundamental law of nature, and certain well-known everyday circumstances of human life. A passage in the 'Property' chapter of the *Second Treatise* will serve as an illustration. A (derivative) law of nature grants to all persons access to the earth and its fruits for their sustenance. For if persons lack such access, they perish. But the fundamental law of nature requires that all are to be preserved as much as may be, and therefore it could not be that people should be denied such access (II.26). Locke's conception of the rational justification of a law of nature is teleological: a derivative law of nature is shown to be rationally necessary in the light of the usual circumstances of human life and a certain end (mankind's preservation).

This interpretation of the manner in which Locke intended to apply the fundamental law of nature is similar to that suggested by A. John Simmons (Simmons 1992, 50):

> the fundamental law of nature is, I think, meant to function in Locke's moral theory much as the principle of utility has been thought to function in some rule-utilitarian schemes. The superstructure of Locke's moral theory, then, is a kind of rule-consequentialism, with the preservation of mankind serving as the 'ultimate end' to be advanced.

It would be anachronistic, of course, to suggest (and Simmons is not suggesting) that Locke was literally a rule-utilitarian. Furthermore, the 'end' which Locke proposes for his scheme is only one amongst a number of human goods. 'Preservation' cannot be presented as an all-inclusive conception of the human good in the way that classical versions of utilitarianism attempted to present 'utility' and 'happiness'.

The claim that this shows how the law of nature is the law of reason is open to objection. How can it be shown that the *end* – mankind's being preserved as much as may be – is rationally required? At this point it would appear that Locke's justification ceases to be 'secular', and comes to depend on a theological postulate. We are the products of God's workmanship.

> For men being all the workmanship of one omnipotent and infi-
> nitely wise maker, all the servants of one sovereign master, sent
> into the world by his order and about his business, they are his
> property whose workmanship they are, made to last during his,
> not one another's, pleasure. (II.6)

Locke thinks it is reasonable to assume that if God created us, then
it is his intention that we should continue to exist for as long as He
chooses, just as we would assume that a painter intended her painting
to continue to exist in the absence of any indication to the contrary.
It therefore follows that no one has a right to destroy themselves; and
from this it further follows that we could not transfer such a right to
another: in particular, to a government.

If the theological premise is granted, Locke can show that it is
rational to accept the fundamental law of nature. Modern political
theory, avoiding the justification of normative political claims on the
basis of theological ones, therefore would reject Locke's understanding of the rationality of the law of nature. Possibly a 'secular'
justification for the claim that mankind should be preserved as much
as may be could be found, but it is not easy to see how this can be
done. More likely, it is just something we (human beings) could be
brought to agree upon (perhaps).

Natural rights are simply rights conferred upon persons by the
laws of nature. Natural rights are conferred by 'derivative' natural
laws, rather than by the fundamental law of nature itself. This is
because the fundamental law of nature only specifies an *end* to be
achieved by the body of natural laws. It does not itself directly state
what precepts we are to follow.

Natural rights seem to be regarded by Locke as rights of control
people have over themselves. They are rights of self-ownership: 'every
man has a property in his own person' (II.27). These rights protect
you in controlling yourself so long as what you do is consistent with
the self-ownership rights of everyone else. It may be wondered how
Locke can make this assertion when he also claims that we are the
property of God. A possible explanation is that Locke is looking at
the question of self-ownership from more than one point of view. From
the standpoint of our relationship with God we are to regard ourselves

as having no more than a 'lease' on our own lives, to be terminated at our Creator's pleasure. This allows Locke to claim that we do *not* have the right to take our own lives, in contrast to a modern defender of self-ownership, who would consider herself bound to defend a right to suicide. However, when each individual is seen from the point of view of every other, Locke seems to regard us as in 'freehold' rather than 'leasehold' possession of ourselves. Such a conception gives strong grounds for why each of us should respect the integrity of every other person. For you to allow that another (mortal) person might have some partial right to control you would be to risk respect for your rights, but no such risk is involved if, ultimately, God owns you.

Though Locke thinks that natural rights take the form of self-ownership rights, he does *not* think that all natural rights are property rights in the ordinary sense. True, by acting in certain ways, Locke believes that a person *can* begin a natural property right in a previously unowned thing (II.27). But not all Lockean natural rights are of this character. For one thing, many natural rights we have under the law of nature do not require any particular event to occur in order for that right to be acquired. The right of the innocent to remain physically unmolested is a right they always have. (We might call this a 'general' natural right, following the usage in Hart 1967, 63ff.) But a natural right to property in a particular thing is (if Locke is to be believed) a right one acquires through the occurrence of a specific event: in this case by acting in a specific way with respect to a specific thing. We could call this a 'particular' natural right. Another example of a particular natural right is your right that a person who has promised you something should do what she has promised. (This usage of 'particular right' is similar to Hart's usage of 'special right' in Hart 1967, 60ff.)

The state of nature

From the point of view of political organization people can be in one of only two stable conditions according to Locke: the state of nature or civil society. To show how the state can be legitimate is, for him, to show how you can get from the state of nature to civil society in a morally unexceptionable way. What is the state of nature like? Locke says that in this state all persons are free, equal and independent (II.4–6). Locke does not mean that they are free to do anything they like. They are not free (morally speaking) to act contrary to the law of nature. In the state of nature people are free to do anything allowed by the law of nature.

The state of nature is a condition in which none of the institutions of the state exist, and hence in which there are no requirements of positive law. What does Locke mean by saying that people are 'equal' in the state of nature? First, he means that everyone in the state of nature has the same set of natural rights (except for children, lunatics and idiots (II.59, 60)). People have these natural rights simply in virtue of being persons. Now legitimate political authority implies moral inequality, in that if one person has political authority over another, then the one with authority has a moral right to the obedience of the other in certain respects. So, for Locke, if there can be justifiable inequalities it must be possible to show how this can be so, starting out from a position of moral equality. The equality of persons in the state of nature also refers to the idea that in the state of nature people are in an equal position to know what the law of nature is, for the law of nature is known by reason, and all 'normal' people have reason.

Now the law of nature sets out what people's relationships ought to be in the state of nature, but it does not say what people in fact will do. The law of nature is, we may recall, a *normative* law – a law concerning what people ought to do, not a law about how events do in fact go. Locke allows that some may violate the natural rights of others. In that event, how do things stand, morally speaking? If someone violates one of your natural rights, not only do you have the right that this should not happen, you also have a 'second-order' natural right to attempt to enforce your first-order right. Locke calls this second-order right the 'executive power of the law of nature' (II.7–13, 74, 87, 105). The existence of this right is crucial to Locke's account of how legitimate political authority can arise. The executive power of the law of nature has three main aspects:

1. The right to judge for yourself what actions are and are not in accordance with the law of nature.

2. The right to restrain attempts to violate the law of nature, using force if necessary.

3. In the case of those who, in the light of your conscientious judgement, have violated the law of nature, the right to judge what is the appropriate punishment, and to attempt to impose that punishment.

The executive power of the law of nature is parasitic upon first-order natural rights. If people did not have first-order natural rights there would be nothing the executive power of the law of nature could be deployed to protect.

A distinction has been implied between a right to use force in the state of nature and a right to punish. It could be allowed that persons have the right to use force in the state of nature in order to beat off attempts to violate their own or others' natural rights without allowing that they have a right to punish. For in order to have the right to punish one must have the right to use force (in addition to any force necessary to constrain would-be rights violators) to impose injury or to incarcerate as retribution for the violation of the law of nature. Indeed sometimes punishment might be appropriate for serious intent to violate the law of nature even when no force was needed for restraint because the attempt to violate the law of nature was too incompetent to need restraining.

Locke offers the following argument for the existence of a right to punish (II.7). The law of nature would be 'in vain' if there were no power to enforce it. God does nothing in vain. Therefore, as God has made such a law there must always be an appropriate power. Now in the state of nature there is no civil power, and therefore the earthly power to enforce the law of nature must lie in the hands of persons as individuals. The standing of persons is equal in the state of nature. Therefore if anyone has the power to enforce the law of nature, everyone must have it. So, everyone has it (with the usual exceptions, such as children and the insane).[1]

The right to use force in the state of nature would appear to be plausible and feasible from the point of view of a defender of natural rights. But the idea of a natural right to punish raises greater difficulties. One of these is that we may think that if someone is said to

21

be *punished* this must involve the application of some *institutional* process, rather than a mere act of will on the part of an individual. Another is that there would seem to be practical difficulties about actually carrying out many forms of punishment (such as custodial sentences) without an institutional structure. These problems arise even if one thinks (which is itself, perhaps, not so plausible) that there are quite clear punishments prescribed in the law of nature for all offences against the law of nature, and that there is no significant conventional element in determining what the punishment for various offences should be.

Locke's reason for postulating the executive power of the law of nature is linked to his main strategy for showing how political authority can be legitimate. Locke assumes that if it can be shown that there is something a government may do with right, then this must be consistent with the natural rights persons had in the state of nature. But not only does Locke require consistency: more demandingly, he requires that any right which may be properly exercised by government should have had its origin in a right individuals would have had in the state of nature. Thus, if the state may, with right, enforce the law of nature, then individuals in the state of nature must have originally had rights, such that the government could have acquired the right to enforce the law of nature upon all of its citizens. And if a state has the authority to punish, that right must have rested with its citizens as individuals. A monopoly of the authority to impose punishments (anyway, serious punishments) might be thought to be part of the definition of a state.

Discussion of Locke's doctrines concerning natural rights is sometimes rather loosely associated with the idea of *inalienable* rights. Indeed some suppose that if a right is natural it must be inalienable. Locke does think that some natural rights are inalienable. You cannot by your own free consent alienate your right to your natural freedom by, say, agreeing to become a slave (II.23). (People can rightfully become slaves, according to Locke, but only as the result of a process of just punishment.) But, as the preceding discussion implies, some natural rights, such as the executive power of the law of nature, must be alienable. For, according to Locke's theory, any right a government has to act must have come from its citizens, and any right *they* have in the state of nature must be a natural right. Therefore, if the right to use force and to impose punishments is to end up in the hands of government, there must be an alienable natural right.

This brings us to the question of why persons in the state of nature should wish to part with their executive power of the law of nature. They do so as part of a strategy to remedy what Locke calls the 'inconveniencies' of the state of nature (II.124–7). These are, first, that each person must be his or her own judge of whether the law of nature has been violated. So in the state of nature a dispute over whether the law of nature has been violated cannot be referred to an impartial authority. It may remain unsettled, and hence cause contention. Second, when, in the state of nature, people take the punishment of alleged violators of the law of nature into their own hands, there is no guarantee that justice will have force on its side. Each person's bias towards his or her own interests is likely to make violators of natural rights seem worse than they really are, and to be an incentive to excessive punishment. The reasons for setting up political society are, therefore, that there should be a single, common, known interpretation of the law of nature by reference to which disputes can be settled, and that there should be standard punishments for the violation of those common rules, impartially administered and enforced. The state is, in effect, a device for ensuring that the law of nature in fact regulates people's relationships with each other. (However, this is not the only thing the state does in Locke's view, as we shall see later.) This leads to Locke's definition of political power.

> Political power, then, I take to be a right of making laws with penalties of death, and consequently all less penalties, for the regulating and preserving of property, and of employing the force of the community in the execution of such laws, and in the defence of the commonwealth from foreign injury, and all this only for the public good. (II.3)

Locke does not mean that political power is to be employed only to protect property in the ordinary sense. He is using the term 'property' in an extended sense, in which it refers to 'all of that over which a person has rights'; i.e. a person's rights over herself as well as over her property in the usual sense.

Now although the law of nature fully applies to everyone in the state of nature, it is another matter whether it is always obeyed. On this point Locke is not altogether consistent. In II.19 he says

> And here we have the plain difference between the state of nature and the state of war, which, however some men have confounded, are as far distant as a state of peace, good-will, mutual assistance, and preservation, and a state of enmity, malice, violence, and mutual destruction are one from another.

But despite this apparent repudiation of Hobbes, only a little later, in II.21, Locke says

> To avoid this state of war (wherein there is no appeal but to heaven, and wherein every the least difference is apt to end, where there is no authority to decide between the contenders) is one great reason of men's putting themselves into society, and quitting the state of nature.

At first Locke appears to be denying Hobbes' view that in the absence of political authority there is no system of moral rules which will succeed in regulating conflict. But later Locke ends up by agreeing with Hobbes on what the state of nature will be like. While, for Locke, moral rules have application to those who are in the state of nature, they are often not followed, and the state of nature in Locke is not so far removed from Hobbes' state of war. One may speculate about the reason for Locke's apparent inconsistency. He does not want to suggest too bad a picture of the state of nature because he wants to argue that there are definite conditions on the state's exercise of political power. That is easier to argue if the state of nature is not such a bad alternative to civil society. On the other hand, Locke does not want the state of nature to be so good that there is no obvious reason why people would ever wish to leave it.

The development of the concept of the executive power of the law of nature is a crucial move in Locke's attempt to show that political authority can exist with moral right. In order for such an authority to exist the executive power of the law of nature must pass out of the hands of individuals and come to be under the control of government, by processes which violate no one's natural rights. Now as Locke assumes that in the state of nature persons are 'owners' of their executive power of the law of nature, there is no way in which these powers can end up in other hands except by each person consenting to such a transfer. Although Locke thinks that there is good reason why the executive power of the law of nature should come to be in the hands of a single authority, that authority would not be legitimate unless the original owners of the executive power of the law of nature consented to relinquish it. Thus Locke is committed to giving a contract argument for legitimate government.

The formation of the community

Locke proposes a two-stage process by which government is formed. In the first stage each person makes a compact with every other wishing to quit the state of nature whereby it is agreed to surrender her executive power of the law of nature, and to make it over to all those (as a collectivity) who have entered this compact (II.14, 95, 171). Each person agrees to surrender individual control over her executive power of the law of nature in exchange for an equal share, along with all the other contractors, in the joint control of everyone's pooled executive power of the law of nature. The executive power of the law of nature is 'de-privatized'.

This new entity now created by the compact Locke calls 'the community' (II.87, 95, 96, 99, 130). The community is a half-way house between the state of nature and the state. It is no longer the state of nature because individual, unilateral control over the executive power of the law of nature has been given up. But it is not yet a state because there is no formally constituted body which has the authority to wield this power; that is, to legislate, and to enforce the law. The concept of the community is one of Locke's most interesting and fertile contributions to political thought. It has been said (Ashcraft 1986, 310) that the doctrine of the community had been around for some time in Whig ideology. It had been used to explain how the people could still have a 'will' if the King had dissolved Parliament, and thereby the body through which the people expressed its will. Their 'will' then lay in the 'community'. It seems difficult to avoid making use of a conception such as Locke's community when considering groups of people who are significant as political entities but who lack formal, sovereign political institutions; such as the peoples of Latvia, Lithuania and Estonia were until recently. However, it is most implausible, of course, that such entities are constituted by voluntary, individual incorporation. On the contrary, the reasons why people would consider themselves members of such a group would be the non-voluntary, acquired characteristics of language, culture and attachment to a homeland. The contrasting 'universalism' and 'rationalism' of Locke's position is evident when one considers that those who enter the compact need be united by nothing but a desire to quit the state of nature, and a common understanding of how this is to be done. Otherwise they need not be related by ethnic considerations, culture or even language.

Perhaps this is to go beyond the conception of the community to be found in Locke. It is true that for Locke the existence of the community is not dependent on the continued existence of an established constitutional government. This explains how 'the same' political entity can persist through a period of political instability and revolution. However, Locke thinks that the situation in which there is a community but no government is *unstable*, and that the community too will dissolve if power is not entrusted quickly to a new constitutional government (II.212). This suggests that in Locke's view (and quite consistently) there is, in the end, nothing to hold the community together but its common resolve to establish civil society. Therefore the use of this notion to describe the continued existence of, say, Latvia as a political entity in the absence of the appropriate political institutions during the Soviet era, is something of an extension, perhaps even a distortion, of the Lockean view.

To return to the main line of argument: the formation of the community leaves things incomplete, and calls for a second stage in order to establish civil society. The parties to the original compact are aiming for a remedy to the 'inconveniencies' of the state of nature: they need a common, agreed interpretation of the law of nature, impartially enforced. So their collective executive power of the law of nature must be exercised by a formally constituted authority. This will be referred to as the 'government', though Locke does not, of course, have in mind a specific administration, but rather a constitutional form of government, such as nowadays would be instanced by the British parliamentary system, or the United States federal presidential and congressional system. These are capable of generating specific administrations in accordance with standing procedures.

The members of the community have to decide into what constitutional form they are to entrust their executive power of the law of nature. It should be noted that the entrustment is to a *constitutional form*, rather than directly to particular persons. The constitutional form will enable us to identify those persons who hold political power with right. They will be the ones who have satisfied the constitutionally prescribed processes for holding legitimate power; for example, being elected. Locke supposes that there are various permissible forms, the basic ones being (constitutional) monarchy, oligarchy and democracy. There will not necessarily be unanimous agreement about which form to adopt. So what procedure is to be used to decide? Locke says that when you agree to the original compact you must be regarded as having agreed, implicitly (as having 'tacitly consented', in one understanding of that expression), to be bound by the majority decision as to where the collectivized executive power of the law of nature is to be entrusted. By majority decision the members of the community entrust their collective executive powers of the law of nature into the hands of a constitutional form of government, and the state, properly speaking, is created.

Democracy

The process by which the collective executive power of the law of nature is entrusted to a form of government is undoubtedly majoritarian in Locke's view (II.95, 99, 176). But the character of the constitution to which that power is entrusted need not be. Constitutions which are not democratic may be chosen by the community, and may be legitimate. *Absolute* monarchy is not legitmate, however, and may not be chosen because it implies that political authority does not rest on the consent of the people. But *constitutional* monarchy is an acceptable choice.

It has been suggested (Simmons 1979, 71–2) that there is some tension in Locke (and in other contract theorists) between individual consent and majority consent. If one requires that *every* individual should consent, then it would appear that consent must be unanimous, and any individual who does not consent is not obligated. This seems to be inconsistent with a doctrine of *majority* consent, in which it is not necessary for every individual to consent personally in order for that individual to be obligated by the consent of the majority.

It is a mistake, however, to suppose that there is any inconsistency in Locke on this issue. For the giving of individual consent and of majority consent are two different things. Individual consent is given to the original compact by which you relinquish your executive power of the law of nature. Everyone who is a member of the civil society has given this consent. If you do not give it, then you are just not in the civil society. Majority consent applies to the decision of a community to entrust its power to a particular government. Here unanimity is not required, and even if you are in the minority you still have consented, according to Locke. For in making the original compact you tacitly consented to be bound by the decision of the majority.

Locke's views on democracy may seem a little strange to us. It may help us to understand them better if we mark the following distinction. First there is the process by which the 'collectivized' executive power of the law of nature is entrusted by the community to a government. Undoubtedly, according to Locke, that process should take place in line with the principles of majoritarian democracy. (However, in accordance with the universal assumption of the time, women would not have been included.) Of course, the process cannot be formalized, as we do not yet have a state; so the institutional structures for a formal majoritarian process (such as a referendum) are not yet in place. But in some unspecified *informal* way the process must be majoritarian. For example, we could say that the last communist government of East Germany was removed by an *informal* majoritarian process. Second, there is the character of that constitution to which the collectivized power is entrusted. For example, the United States federal constitution is democratic; the British constitution is somewhat less so, in that it has an unelected second chamber and an unelected head of state, and the constitution of seventeenth-century

Venice was not at all democratic, but an oligarchy of the nobility. Locke thinks that people may decide to entrust their power to a democratic form of government if they wish, but they do not have to do this.

It may be thought that at this point Locke departs from the natural logic of his own position. Given the way in which Locke constructs the community, it would seem that there is clear reason why the constitutional form of government should be democratic. For, it may be argued, each party to the compact has contributed something of equal weight, his or her executive power of the law of nature. As after the compact they may no longer decide how to deploy their portion of the collective power unilaterally (except in life-threatening emergencies), the obvious way to control the collective executive power of the law of nature is for each to have an equal share in deciding how it is to be exercised.

This is one of those fascinating points in the development of a political theory where its natural implications are not pursued by its author because of the seeming absurdity of the implications, as seen from the point of view of the acceptable political beliefs of the time. To have suggested, in late seventeenth-century Europe, that only a democratic government elected on a universal adult franchise was legitimate, would have invited ridicule from one's opponents. Of course this (for Locke) embarrassing apparent implication of his theory can only add to its credibility for us. If Locke had made such a revision to his theory it would have simplified the problems he has about how to determine when the majority of the community has withdrawn its consent. This point will be considered in the chapter on rebellion.

That said, it remains true, of course, that Locke asserts that in the last resort political power lies in the hands of the people. This, as has been argued (Ashcraft 1986, 300), is a doctrine having radical enough implications in Locke's own day. For 'the people' will be all those with natural rights, and they will consist mostly of 'the lower orders', for example, tradesmen, shopkeepers, craftsmen, servants and agricultural labourers. Locke is saying, in effect, that it is a majority of *these* that constitute the ultimate repository of political power. Now in a society where most of even the leading radicals took it entirely for granted that political affairs were the domain of the 'better sort of people' (i.e. those of property, education and leisure), this was a very advanced view.

One Tory (George Hicks in 1682) did indeed point out, quite correctly, that the natural law doctrine of the Whig radicals implied that there should be votes for women. For women are as much rational beings subject to the law of nature as men, and therefore their consent to government should matter just as much. This point seems to have been advanced by Hicks in the spirit of having produced a *reductio ad absurdum* refutation of the natural law view (Ashcraft 1986, 236).

Locke's position on the role of the majority in legitimizing political power is ingenious from the point of view of dealing with certain internal divisions within the Whig party. As has already been mentioned, the *Second Treatise* was not written as an academic text, but as a contribution to the political life of the time. Locke sought to avoid the wanton alienation of possible sources of support for the revolutionary cause, and his position about the majority is, as now will be explained, ingenious from that point of view.

It has been said (Ashcraft 1986, 237) that the Whigs were apt to be evasive about who 'the people' were. This was to avoid opening up divisions within the Whig party, whose supporters included aristocrats and gentry who were not keen on extending the franchise, as well as the unenfranchised poor. Now Locke is saying that ultimately political power rests with the people, and therefore it is altogether proper that they should participate, as primary agents, in a revolution. It is not appropriate, nor is it required, that the 'lower orders' should stand to one side and allow questions of legitimacy to be decided by their 'betters'. Thus the 'lower orders', amongst whom the Whigs had considerable support, were guaranteed a place in the most fundamental political processes. Legitimate government depended upon *their* consent (as well as that of others). However, many upper-class and influential Whigs (including Shaftesbury) were opposed to any extension of the franchise. To them Locke could say that the place occupied by the people in the fundamental process of legitimizing government did not imply that the system of government itself had to be democratic. Thus the influential Whigs, who were reluctant to share political power more widely, did not have their position challenged by Locke's theory. Anyway, so long as it could be claimed that the people had chosen to entrust political power to the very restrictedly democratic system of government that then prevailed, the 'lower orders' could support the revolution without it necessarily being an injustice to them that they should have no formal power or influence in the post-revolutionary government.

The institution of government

To return to the outline of Locke's main theory of the legitimacy of the state: the first step in the process which leads to the establishment of legitimate political authority is the 'pooling' of the executive power of the law of nature. That is a matter of individuals contracting. Locke does not regard the next stage as a contract. The community (strictly, a majority of the community) place their pooled executive power of the law of nature in the hands of the government *on trust* (II.149). Locke is not advocating a double contract theory – first, a contract between each individual and every other, and second, a contract between the people collectively and the government-to-be. For Locke the only contract is that between you and each of your fellow citizens to give up individual control of your respective executive powers of the law of nature. If you fail to obey your legitimate government the obligation you ignore is one owed to your fellow citizens rather than to the government directly.

Why does Locke make the second step a trust rather than a compact? Earlier it was said that Locke intends his core theory to show both how government can be legitimate and how it can be legitimately rebelled against. The second intention bears on the present point. If there were a second contract the people as a collective, i.e. the community, would have rights against the government if it violated the terms of the contract, but similarly the government would have rights against the people. In a dispute between the government and the people there would be nobody to turn to for adjudication. But if government has its power only on trust from the people, then the people have the right to withdraw that power whenever it pleases them to do so. For Locke the power government exercises always belongs to the people, and a legitimate government has its power only on trust from them (II.240).

It may be doubted whether it is Locke's opinion that the people, as a collective, have the right to withdraw their power whenever it pleases them. Is it not Locke's view that the people may rebel only when the government has breached the trust that the people have placed in it? The people have placed their power in the hands of the government on the understanding that the government will use it to define and enforce everyone's natural rights, and to further the common good. Now it is true that Locke thinks the people would wish to withdraw their power only if they believed that this trust had been broken. But ultimately it is up to the people to judge, and there is no one (on earth) who can sit in judgement on *them*, and say whether they have *properly* judged on whether the trust has been broken. In effect, therefore, they may withdraw the trust whenever it pleases them. This point, too, will be discussed further in the chapter on rebellion.

Corresponding to these two stages in the process by which legitimate government is established there are, for Locke, two senses in which government rests on consent. First, each individual consents to the original compact by which he divests himself of the executive power of the law of nature. Here consent is contractual. One agrees to give up a right to something which in the state of nature is one's own, and to transfer it to the community, on condition that everyone else does likewise. Second, government rests on the consent of the people; that is, on the consent of a majority of the people, to the continuance of that trust whereby the government has the right to exercise the executive power of the law of nature (II.134). Here consent is *not* contractual. I shall adopt the term *attitudinal* for this kind of consent (from Simmons 1979, 93, 97).

Attitudinal consent to something is a matter of how one feels about it, rather than a matter of what one undertakes to do with respect to it. If the non-smokers really do not care about the smokers smoking, then they have given their attitudinal consent to the smokers smoking. Attitudinal consent may be present where there has been no contract. Although the non-smokers may not have given any formal agreement to the smokers smoking, they still may be said to consent in the attitude they take. Also, contractual consent may exist where there is no attitudinal consent. If the non-smokers formally agree to allow the smokers to smoke, then they are obliged to put up with smoking in accordance with the agreement, even though they hate it; i.e. even though they do not give their attitudinal consent. It might be wondered why anyone would give their genuine (i.e. free) contractual consent to something when they did not give their attitudinal consent to it. The most obvious reason would be the expectation of gaining something through doing a deal. If the non-smokers agree to the smokers being allowed to smoke then the smokers might agree to co-operate in some task which the non-smokers want done, and which only can be done with the co-operation of smokers and non-smokers.

This distinction between two kinds of consent has a natural logic if we consider how it fits in with other parts of Locke's theory. The consent given by the community to entrusting power to a particular system of government cannot be a matter of individuals contracting, because it is the body of persons, not individuals as such, who do the entrusting. However, the consent involved cannot be the contractual consent of the body of persons who comprise the community. This is because the community is not a formally incorporated body, with persons empowered to act on its behalf, in the way in which the chief administrators of a college may be empowered to act on the college's behalf. The stage of formal incorporation will be reached only when the power *is* entrusted to a system of government. This leaves little alternative to the suggestion that the consent the community is capable of giving as a body to the entrusting of its power is attitudinal consent.

We can summarize Locke's position by reviewing the progress from the state of nature to political authority. There are three stages. In the first, the state of nature, each person has the right to control his or her own executive power of the law of nature. The second is the community, which comes after the contract 'collectivizing' the executive power of the law of nature, but before the collective power has been entrusted to a system of government. The third is the commonwealth. By this stage the community, by majority vote, has entrusted its executive power of the law of nature to a system of government, for it to exercise on the community's behalf so long as the trust continues. The state vests this power in the appropriate institutions, the legislative, the executive and the judicial, and a political order, properly speaking, now exists.

Is Locke's argument for political authority successful?
Tacit consent

The exposition of Locke's 'core' account of the 'normative' emergence of the state is now complete. Does it succeed in showing how legitimate government is possible? First let us review Locke's answer to the question 'Why ought you to obey your government if it enjoys the attitudinal consent of the majority of your fellow citizens to the continuance of the trust they have placed in it?' (It might help to imagine that the context is one where you can see no moral legitimacy whatsoever in what your government is requiring of you. In Britain recently many regarded the requirement to pay the poll tax in this way.) Locke answers as follows. You have consented, individually and contractually, to making over to the community the executive power of the law of nature which you controlled as an individual in the state of nature. In consenting to that you consented tacitly (that is, by implication) to be bound by the majority's decision as to where the power of the community was to be vested. Now the community has entrusted that power to the particular form of government we have, and has not withdrawn that trust. Therefore you are bound to obey the government, and it rightfully exercises the executive power of the law of nature over you, so long as the majority of the community continues to place that trust in it. Thus you may be under an obligation to obey the legislation of a legitimate government even when you are opposed to that legislation. If you thought that the legislation actually violated the law of nature (as some opponents of the poll tax did), then the situation is different and more complicated, as we shall see later.

A necessary condition for this argument to work is that all those properly subject to the state must be shown to have given their contractual consent to the original compact. Locke is quite explicit about this. 'Men being, as has been said, by nature all free, equal and independent, no man can be put out of this estate and subjected to the political power of another without his own consent' (II.95). Even if it were credible that there was an original compact, this would show nothing about the obligations of the present generation. ' 'Tis true that whatever engagements or promises anyone has made for himself, he is under the obligation of them, but cannot by any compact whatsoever bind his children or posterity' (II.116). So if the present government is legitimate, members of the present generation must have consented in some way or other to it. But it is implausible that there could be universal express consent. It is implausible that every adult subject to government would have sworn some appropriate oath. Many or most members of the present generation must, then, have 'tacitly' consented to the original compact.

Before moving on, it may be recalled that Locke uses the expression 'tacit consent' in at least one other way. The case encountered earlier is that where Locke says that if you consent to the original compact then you can be taken to have 'tacitly consented' to be bound by the majority decision as to where the 'pooled' executive power of the law of nature is to be entrusted. This use of 'tacit consent' can be explained as follows. If you consent expressly to P, then you can be said to tacitly consent to Q, if it would be generally taken that consenting to P involves consenting to Q. For example, if you expressly consent to enter a competition, then you consent to the possibility that you might not win, for there must be losers in competitions. In the example in Locke, he is suggesting that you must (by implication) consent to be bound by majority decision when you make the original compact. For otherwise (if you insisted on unanimity, for example) the intention of the contractors to establish a political society probably would be thwarted, for it is most unlikely that the pooled executive power of the law of nature would ever be entrusted to a system of government unanimously.

It is not *this* conception of tacit consent that I wish to question. In this sense it is plausible that in expressly consenting to some things we tacitly consent to others. But this cannot help Locke with the idea of tacit consent to the original compact. For 'tacit consent' in the sense of 'implied consent' must always follow express consent to something else. But in the case of the original compact we have, *ex hypothesi*, the first or original consenting. Locke is looking for some act the performance of which, though it would not count as the giving of express consent, would bind us to relinquishing our executive power of the law of nature just as if there had been an act of express consent.

In the discussion so far it is, of course, being assumed that persons can become full members of the commonwealth and citizens of the state (as contrasted with merely being subject to the state's laws, as in the case of a tourist, for example) by giving their tacit consent. But this would seem to be clearly contrary to the view Locke expresses in II.122.

> And thus we see that foreigners, by living all their lives under another government, and enjoying the privileges and protection of it, though they are bound, even in conscience, to submit to its administration, as far forth as any denizen, yet do not thereby come to be subjects or members of that commonwealth. Nothing can make any man so, but his actually entering into it by positive engagement, and express promise and compact.

Now if what the foreigner does amounts to giving his tacit consent, then it would seem that Locke is denying that tacit consent can make you a member of the commonwealth (though it does result in your having an obligation to obey the laws of the commonwealth). The passage quoted appears to make it quite clear that only express consenters are full members of the commonwealth.

However, this interpretation is also unsatisfactory. Locke does not say what is to count as express consent. But on any reasonable understanding of what is to count (swearing a solemn oath, or making a declaration in writing, for example), very few would become full members of the commonwealth on this criterion. It is very implausible to suppose that Locke wished to confine membership of the commonwealth to so few. Furthermore, when Locke introduces his distinction between express and tacit consent in II.119, he can be read as implying that tacit consent is one way in which a person can become a subject of a government. Less direct evidence for my view is supplied by Ruth Grant (Grant 1987, 123–4). Locke allows that in earlier times the power of a father over his children during their minority may have been converted almost imperceptibly into monarchical power. Locke insists, though, that paternal power and monarchical power are still not the same, and says that for the exercise of monarchical power to have become legitimate the children must have given their express or tacit consent to it upon coming of age (II.74–5, 94, 110). Here Locke clearly implies that one may become a member of a commonwealth by giving one's tacit consent.

Another attempt to understand Locke's position on express and tacit consent rests on his views concerning the inheritance of property in II.73. There Locke claims that there is 'always annexed to the enjoyment of land a submission to the government of the country of which that land is a part'. (Locke's position on this point is further elaborated in II.120.) Locke says that this is commonly (but mistakenly) supposed to imply that 'a father could oblige his posterity to that government of which he himself was a subject'. The actual situation, Locke tells us, is that the beneficiary has the choice whether to accept the inheritance or not (and hence the condition that attaches to it, i.e. submission to the appropriate government). Now it might be suggested that this is what Locke understands by 'express consent'; i.e. the consent given by the recipient of an inheritance, with the attached implication of submission.

There are, however, difficulties with this interpretation also. First, referring back to what was said a little earlier about 'tacit consent', where this is consent implied by the giving of express consent to something else – we see that the present case is, for Locke, one that fits that pattern, and is therefore a case of *tacit* consent to government. For *express* consent is given to the acceptance of the inheritance, and the consent to submission to the government under whose jurisdiction the estate falls is tacit consent. This interpretation of Locke's view is confirmed by what he says in II.121. One who has the enjoyment of land is said to submit to the government under whose jurisdiction the land lies only so long as the enjoyment continues. This, Locke says, is *tacit* consent, and the landholder is at liberty, if he sells his possession, to incorporate himself into some other commonwealth. Then, in II.122, Locke goes on to say that to be a member of a society and a perpetual subject of a commonwealth depends on 'positive engagement, and express promise and compact'. It remains a mystery what this 'express compact' can consist of.

It seems clear from II.62 that Locke would regard 'oaths of fealty, or allegiance' to be instances of express consent, but this would seem to cover too few members of a commonwealth to constitute the only way in which full consent can be given.

Some (e.g. Macpherson 1962, 248–51) have suggested that Locke held that the inheritors of land expressly consent and are full members of the commonwealth, while the propertyless merely tacitly consent and are required to obey the laws, while not being full members of the commonwealth, or having any right to participate in its political life. It will be clear from the foregoing discussion that this interpretation rests on a misreading of Locke's position.

I am unable to propose a reading of Locke on this point which is consistent with all of the relevant passages. However, the situation is sufficiently ambiguous for it to be reasonable to continue on the assumption that Locke did think that one could become a member of a commonwealth by giving one's tacit consent. Simmons (1993, 80–90) has a meticulous discussion of the issue.

What act do we perform, then, that is the giving of this tacit consent? Locke's answer is given in the latter part of Chapter VIII of the *Second Treatise* (II.116ff.). The arguments shortly to be given against tacit consent are unaffected by exactly what Locke thought constituted the giving of tacit consent. But perhaps the most plausible interpretation of Locke on this point is that you give your tacit consent to the terms of the original compact by simply being within the territories of a certain state, i.e. by being in possession of, or by enjoying, any part of the dominions of any government (II.119).

Two common objections are made to Locke's position, interpreted in this way. First, Locke appears to suppose that tacit consent can be given unintentionally, simply by being within the territories of a government, even if a person does not consciously suppose that she is consenting. But surely it is implausible that binding contractual consent should be given unintentionally, the person giving the supposed consent being unaware that this is what she will be taken to be doing in acting in a certain way. Second, for an act to constitute binding contractual consent, that consent must be given freely. A person must have the choice of performing or not performing the act whereby consent is given. But many people, because of financial and other constraints, do not have any real option of leaving the territories of the government they are under. This is assuming that they are legally permitted to leave, and that there are other countries which would accept them as immigrants. This was pointed out by David Hume in his essay *Of the Original Contract* (Hume 1987).

These two objections have a limited impact on Locke's project. True, they rule out 'being within the territories' as that 'act' the performance of which constitutes the giving of one's tacit consent. However, they do not necessarily rule out Locke's leading idea that political obligation is founded on tacit consent. Perhaps there is some better choice that could be made of what is to count as that act the performance of which constitutes the giving of one's tacit consent. At this point, however, a more comprehensive argument against Locke can be proposed. It will be argued that it is impossible that there should be an act that could fit the role Locke has in mind. There is nothing that could constitute the giving of one's tacit consent.

This is the reason for saying that there is nothing that could constitute the giving of one's tacit consent to the terms of the original compact. Either an act is recognized (in virtue of some operative convention) as the giving of a person's contractual consent or it is not. If it is so recognized then it is an instance of express consent. This is provided it is performed against the appropriate background conditions; namely, that the act is done freely, and that the agent knows that the act will be taken as indicating consent. Of course not all forms of express consent are verbal or written. Nodding agreement, or failing to indicate one's dissent can, in the appropriate circumstances, constitute express consent. Possibly the fact that some forms of express consent are indicated by inaction in the appropriate circumstances (for example, remaining silent when people are asked whether they agree) made Locke suppose that there could be tacit consent. A. John Simmons gives an example in which the Chairman of the Board asks whether there are any objections to a change of time for the next meeting. The Board members remain silent, and Simmons says that in doing so they give their tacit consent to the change (Simmons 1979, 80). But it is more plausible to say that there is a convention amongst the members of the Board that silence shall be understood to mean agreement. This is an instance of express consent, therefore, where the consent is expressed by inactivity at the appropriate point in the meeting.

If the act is not recognized as the giving of contractual consent, there is no reason for supposing that it constitutes the giving of any kind of consent at all. Now by no act recognized in our operative conventions as an act of contractual consent do we consent to the terms of the original compact. Suppose, however, it is claimed that there *is* an operative convention to the effect that being within the territories of a state implies the giving of one's *express* consent. It is true that Locke's argument now would have to be interpreted as having the form of an express consent argument. But there is no reason why this should be of concern to Locke, so long as he can show that there is consent. Now it is true that other political philosophers have held that residence implies consent, for example, Rousseau (Rousseau 1913, 88, n. 1). But it is difficult to see how it could be claimed seriously that there is such a convention, because in no other area of social life do we take location, as such, to imply consent to something. Whenever spatial location is taken to imply consent to something, there must be a specific understanding that makes it so. Perhaps, though, it could be argued that in Locke's view the state was founded by express compact, and that at the founding a convention was instituted by which residence was to be regarded as the giving of consent by later generations. But this would be to assert that a certain convention had been adopted without producing any historical evidence at all that this was so.

Thus the first step in Locke's argument for legitimate political authority fails. It is true that there are cases where it is uncertain whether an act of the kind called for by an operative convention has or has not been performed. There are hesitant, ambiguous, incompetent and diffident performances, concerning which it is difficult to say whether they are or are not acts of the required kind. But these are not cases of tacit consent as required by Locke. They are cases where there is doubt about whether there has been express consent.

There is another case which might be mistaken for tacit consent. As has already been implied, that act (or that set of acts) the performance of which in appropriate circumstances constitutes the giving of contractual consent is such in virtue of operative conventions. (It may be that, *given* we have the concept of contractual consent, the appropriateness of certain background conditions (for example, that the act is performed freely) is *non-conventional*. But that a certain act, such as affixing one's signature, is a sign of contractual consent is a matter of convention. It is conceivable, for example, that signing might cease to indicate contractual consent, and that keying a personal code into a computer should take over that role.) Conventions of this kind come into and pass out of currency. So there could be situations where it is uncertain whether a convention passing out of use is or is not still operative. Hence there could be doubt about whether the performance of a certain act constitutes the giving of contractual consent. However, this possibility does not help Locke. What Locke needs for tacit consent is *both* that there should be no act which, by an established convention, is clearly the giving of consent, *and* that contractual consent clearly should have been given. It is impossible that both of these requirements should be met.

Some have been attracted by the proposal that if one votes, or even if one has the right to vote, one may be said to have given one's tacit consent or 'quasi-consent' (Singer 1973, 51–2). If it is claimed that by actually voting one gives one's tacit consent, this will not serve Locke as a suitable ground for tacit consent. For Locke's own position does not require that everyone who is obliged to obey a legitimate government votes, or even has the right to vote. The enfranchisement of women was scarcely conceived of in Locke's day, and even if it is true that Locke favoured an extended franchise for men, it was not a universal male franchise. So for Locke tacit consent could not have rested either on actually voting or on having the right to vote.

It might be suggested, however, that a 'modern' Lockean could make use of actual voting, or of having the right to vote, as a basis for tacit consent. The thought is that there is a suitable basis here for tacit consent, even though Locke did not grasp it because he was too limited by the political assumptions of his day. Even this proposal, however, proves not to be acceptable. We cannot say that actual voting is the basis for tacit consent, for not all who are deemed to be politically obliged trouble to vote. This proposal also has the unacceptable implication that a person could avoid acquiring political obligations by refusing to vote. Nor will it do to say that having the right to vote is the basis for tacit consent. For then the ground for saying that one had tacitly consented would be a state of affairs that came about quite independently of one's choice. But the basis of tacit consent must be an act that one has the choice whether to perform or not.

Alternatives to tacit consent

However, this might be thought not to exhaust the possibilities of a contract theory on the Lockean model, even if it exhausts the possibilities of the contract theory Locke actually provided. It seems that a neo-Lockean argument could justify an obligation to obey a possible state, even if not any as yet existing state. This would be a state whose authority was based on the express contractual consent of its citizens in accordance with currently operative conventions. Some citizens of some countries, in becoming naturalized, take oaths of allegiance, and it is reasonable to regard this as a form of express consent. Why should we not extend such a requirement to all citizens? Would we not then have a state which rested on contractual consent? Locke, of course, does not consider such a possibility. Nevertheless, it might be thought to be a possible variation on the basic Lockean approach. In this way, it might be said, anarchism could be refuted on the basis Locke has supplied for us, even if it could not be shown that legitimate authority was to be found in any existing state.

Now we can envisage an organization that exercises authority based on the express contractual consent of all of its members. But, it will be argued, such an organization could not be a state; nor could it perform the functions that Locke wants a state to perform.

For Locke the point of entering civil society is that everyone's natural rights should be better respected than they were in the state of nature. This requires that a political authority should enjoy a monopoly of coercive power over a certain territory. For suppose everyone in a certain territory could choose whether they placed themselves under some political authority or remained independent. And suppose further that if they did opt for political authority they could choose which of a number of authorities it would be. This seems to be a possibility left open by Locke's theory. For although you and all those with whom you have made the compact have to accept a single authority, it does not follow that the person next door will have made a compact with the same group of people as you have. In this situation the 'inconveniencies' of the state of nature will remain with us. For if you have a dispute with your neighbour you might find that she has chosen to put herself under no political authority, or under a different one from yours. Then there will be no impartial authority rightfully claiming jurisdiction over both of you, and to whom you can both appeal. So if you see political authority as having the purpose Locke ascribes to it, then there must be only one political authority in a given territory, and everyone in that territory must be subject to that authority. It would be an extraordinary coincidence if individual contractual consent ever did give rise to any territorial monopolies of coercive power.

Robert Nozick (Nozick 1974, 108ff.) envisages such a situation, but argues that certain forces would come into play producing a tendency to monopoly and a 'dominant protective association'. This may be so, but it would not affect the difficulty raised for Locke's position. For Locke envisages a direct passage from the unassociated individuals of the state of nature to the formation of the community. Locke does not suppose that the first compact proves unsatisfactory (because it fails to result in a monopoly of power within a certain territory), and that therefore it must be followed by further compacts which do lead to a monopoly.

There are places where Locke appears to be quite aware that the possibility just described is an implication of a doctrine of individual contractual consent. 'This [i.e. the making of the original compact] any number of men may do, because it injures not the freedom of the rest; they are left as they were, in the liberty of the state of nature' (II.95). But he does not seem to appreciate that this conflicts with the requirement that political authority, if it is to fulfil the tasks he has in mind for it, must enjoy a territorial monopoly of coercive power. Locke is caught in a conflict between his reason for instituting civil society, and his insistence that legitimate authority can arise only on the basis of individual consent. The present argument shows that it is impossible that the state, which must claim a monopoly of coercive power over a given territory, should have its authority justified in terms of individual contractual consent. It is interesting, in this regard, that Locke does not expressly incorporate the idea of a monopoly of coercive power into his definition of political power (II.3).

Is the contract argument redundant?

We now turn to yet a further possibility. This new view allows that Locke's attempt at a contract argument fails. However, it says that the contract argument was in any case redundant. The suggestion is that Locke could have reached the conclusion he desires directly from certain premises he proposes, without making use of the idea of a contract.

There are several variants of this approach. Here is the first. Suppose that you and I are the only inhabitants of the state of nature. If (in your view) I violate the law of nature, you do not need my consent before you may, with right, attempt to enforce it upon me. Now suppose a group of people form an association in order to enforce the law of nature more effectively. (We could suppose that this group came together through the operation of individual contractual consent. But it is not necessary to suppose that the group came together in this way. It is assumed that the group numbers less than all the people who are around in that part of the state of nature.) Again I, who have remained outside this group, violate the law of nature (in the eyes of the group), and the group, acting concertedly, enforces it upon me. Why can't the group do this with right, and without my consent, if one person can? Locke need only have required of government that it use the people's collective power to enforce the law of nature. The contractual consent of those subject to the enforcement is unnecessary.

On this view a government would be a group of people who act in a concerted fashion to enforce the law of nature, with the justification that each possesses the executive power of the law of nature as an individual. Such groups would, in due course, 'carve out' their respective territories as against the territories of other rule-enforcing bodies. What would be the position of ordinary 'citizens' on this view? They would be people who acquiesced in their 'government' enforcing the law of nature, and who did not bother to exercise their own executive power of the law of nature in an independent way. It surely must be permissible for a person to so acquiesce, in Locke's view. You do not have an obligation to insist on your independent exercise of the executive power of the law of nature even when you have not divested yourself of it by contract.

Locke discusses a case something like this in II.74–6. He considers to what extent a father's authority over his children, when they are still in their minority, might be converted into a form of political authority. After the children have reached their majority a father no longer has a right to the obedience of his children, according to Locke (as we saw earlier). Nevertheless he might become a kind of 'Prince' over his adult children, because the children might acquiesce in the continued exercise of the executive power of the law of nature by the father. Locke thinks that this situation is legitimate, even if there has been no transfer of the executive power of the law of nature from the adult children to the father. (A similar example is found in II.105.)

Locke does allow that a body may enforce the law of nature on people without those people having consented to this. In II.9 Locke says that if the state punishes an alien for a crime, then the right of the authorities in that country to punish cannot have derived from the alien having consented to the original compact upon which the society is based. (Here it appears that Locke thinks it is obvious that the alien is not a member of that civil society. But if simply being within the territories of a state is sufficient to give one's tacit consent, it is not obvious why the 'alien' is not in fact a member of that civil society.) However, Locke actually says that the authorities have the right to punish the alien for violating the law of nature. This is not because the alien has *de facto* become a member of that civil society by temporary residence. It is because of the right the authorities have under the executive power of the law of nature *vis-à-vis* an outsider. In that case, it might be asked, why shouldn't any authority have the right to use collective force (so long as it *is* enforcing the law of nature) irrespective of whether individuals have consented to part with their executive power of the law of nature?

Despite all this Locke does not adopt this strategy as his general theory of the state. There are at least two good reasons for his position. One is that such an approach would give a government an insufficiently extensive right to demand compliance. On this view a government would have no *right* to a monopoly of coercive power. Those who chose to exercise their executive power of the law of nature unilaterally would have a perfect right to do so. No one, including the government, would have the right to stop them. Your judgement of what the law of nature required would be on a par, morally speaking, with the verdicts of the processes of the state. But Locke says:

> there and there only is political society where every one of the members hath quitted this natural power [i.e. the executive power of the law of nature], resigned it up into the hands of the community ... all private judgement of every particular member being excluded, the community comes to be umpire. (II.87).

So Locke might be thought to need something more to show how a state has a right to monopolize enforcement of the law of nature. Even if the state succeeded in intimidating all of its citizens to such an extent that they accepted its interpretation of the law of nature, this would not be the same as enforcing its interpretation with right.

A further problem with the lack of a right to a monopoly of coercive power is the possibility of competing bodies attempting to enforce the law of nature. Any one of these bodies would have as good a right to make the attempt as any other. They might well not have the same view of what the law of nature required. So the situation could be even worse than Locke describes it as being in the state of nature, where only the conflicting views of individuals are set against each other. A monopoly of the right to interpret and enforce the law of nature on the part of the state remains essential for Locke.

The other reason Locke would not wish to accept this approach is that it gives the citizens too little right. It does not result in the government having sufficiently strong obligations towards its citizens. As the government would not have anything that 'belonged' to the people (i.e. the pooled executive power of the law of nature) it would owe nothing to them. The only hold the people have over the government, on this view, is that the government would be obliged to enforce the law of nature.

It has been pointed out by some commentators that at several points Locke's position is closer to Hobbes' than he (Locke) would wish to acknowledge. The present is one. According to Hobbes (Hobbes 1968, 189–90), in the state of nature one has a right (under the Hobbesian law of nature) to do whatever is necessary for one's preservation. As everyone in the Hobbesian state of nature has such a right, and as scarcity prevails, there are conflicts of right in the state of nature. Both you and I have a right in the state of nature to eat the last apple, which each of us desires for our preservation. This situation gives rise to the state of war, and to the need for a sovereign power.

The position would appear to be different in Locke, where the law of nature is intended to be a moral law. But in the Lockean state of nature everyone has a right to attempt to enforce upon others her view of what the law of nature requires (under the executive power of the law of nature). Now these views of what the law of nature requires may, of course, conflict, which is the main reason why a sovereign power is necessary. But no one (prior to the original compact) has a monopoly right to enforce her own view of what the law of nature requires. So if you and I have different views of what the law of nature requires in a particular case, we each have the right to enforce our respective views. Thus Locke's position has the potential to generate a situation with similarities to Hobbes'. The rights of one person in the state of nature may come into conflict with the rights of another, and there may be no peaceful way to resolve the conflict while remaining in the state of nature.

A second attempt may be made to show that Locke did not need his contract argument to establish that there could be legitimate political authority. As we saw earlier, Locke thinks that the foundation of non-fundamental natural laws and natural rights is the fundamental law of nature, 'man being to be preserved, as much as possible' (II.16). More specific natural laws, like that requiring you to do nothing to harm the innocent life of another, are derived from the fundamental law of nature. Now clearly Locke thinks that people will be better preserved in a commonwealth with a legitimate government than in the state of nature. Therefore one might argue directly from the fundamental law of nature that everyone ought to quit the state of nature and enter the commonwealth, for we are all required by that law to do whatever is necessary for our collective preservation. If this argument is correct there is no need for each person to consent to transferring his or her executive power of the law of nature to the community.

There is evidence that this is how Locke thought at an earlier stage in the development of his ideas. John Dunn (Dunn 1984, 31) quotes from an unpublished manuscript of Locke's written in 1678.

> If he finds that God has made him and other men in a state wherein they cannot subsist without society, can he but conclude that he is obliged and that God requires him to follow those rules which conduce to the preserving of society?

This may suggest that Locke thinks that there is no need for individual contractual consent: that we are subject to a direct obligation to follow those rules necessary for the existence of a political society. (Though it must be allowed that Locke may be intending to refer only to natural law in this passage, in which case it would no longer support the interpretation that has been placed upon it.)

A related point is raised by A. John Simmons (Simmons 1992, 62–7). In this instance the context is Essay 4 of the *Essays on the Law of Nature*, where Locke says that natural law requires that we should 'procure and preserve a life in society with other men'. This raises the question of whether Locke means that we have an obligation to attempt to live sociably in the state of nature before the formation of political society, or whether he means that we have an obligation to attempt to create political society (if it does not yet exist), or to maintain it, if it does already exist. If we have a direct obligation under the law of nature to sustain political society, and if we find ourselves already in civil society, this would seem to make a contract giving rise to such an obligation unecessary. Simmons (1992, 66) believes that it would be misleading to suppose that by 'society' Locke here means 'political society'. However, it remains true that for Locke there must be reason under the fundamental law of nature to enter specifically political society as well as pre-political society, for Locke believes that legitimate political society enhances the prospects for the preservation of mankind.

Whatever may be the truth about the interpretation of these passages, it is entirely clear that by the time the *Second Treatise* was written Locke makes individual contractual consent indispensable to his theory. There is good reason why he should do this. He wants to show that a government which has been instituted in the appropriate way, and which honestly tries to enforce the law of nature has *authority* over its citizens. Now arguments concerned with the good consequences of obedience to the state, even if they are quite plausible on factual grounds, cannot show that the state has authority. This is because of a feature of the concept of political authority. You do not show that a person, or a body of persons, has authority over you by pointing out the good consequences of obedience. It may be that you will get along much more peacefully if you accede to the 'requests' of the local mobsters, but the fact that there will be these better consequences does not establish that the mobsters have any real authority over you.

To show that some person or body has authority over you, you do not point to the good consequences of obedience. You point to something which is the ground or basis for obedience. An example would be that when you took up employment you gave an undertaking to work in accordance with the manager's instructions. In order to establish that authority exists one must refer to something that has already taken place – to some 'past-regarding' consideration: not to something about the future – to what the consequences can be expected to be. This is what Locke had hoped to accomplish with his contract argument. Political authority is to be established by way of tracing it back to something that you have done (the giving of your tacit consent), rather than by pointing to the good consequences of good government, namely, the better enforcement of the law of nature.

Political obligation

The failure of Locke's contract argument is therefore of considerable significance for the way in which we view our relationship to the state. (In what follows it is assumed that we are considering a 'decent' state. It is not one which wantonly violates the rights of many of its citizens, or cynically exploits them for the benefit of a privileged class.)

The failure of Locke's argument still leaves us with the possibility of a successful consequentialist argument for the habit of obedience to a certain state. There still may be good consequentialist reasons, in terms of peace and order, for our having a disposition to avoid certain things because they are against the law: for behaving *as if* the state had authority. But the failure of Locke's argument strictly speaking rules out the possibility of a successful argument for the *authority* of the state, authority not being only a matter of justifiable general obedience.

An objection to this line of thought must now be considered. Suppose the truth of what has been said about political authority and consequentialist arguments is granted. Why should it be supposed that the only way in which genuine political authority can be created is through making a contract? We are subject to many moral obligations that exist independent of our wills, such as the obligation to respect the persons of others, and the obligation to do such things as we have given undertakings to do. These obligations are 'there all the time'. Why shouldn't political obligations be the same? Why should we be so confident of the 'artificiality' of political obligation – a confidence characteristic of the social contract tradition?

It would appear that other strategies are available to someone who wants to argue for the authority of the state – strategies that do not call for a contract. In order to set out what some of these might be, let us introduce a distinction between 'general' and 'particular' obligations, parallel to that between 'general' and 'particular' natural rights, used in the section on natural law and natural rights earlier in this chapter. An example of a general obligation would be the obligation to respect the physical integrity of other persons. This is an obligation all persons may be thought to have with respect to all other persons, in the absence of special considerations (e.g. the need to repel assault). There is nothing special that you have to *do* in order to have this obligation. You have it simply in virtue of being a normal human being. Particular obligations are obligations you incur as a result of some particular episode or event in your history. They are not obligations you have in any case, simply in virtue of being a person.

One sub-class of particular obligations is voluntary obligations. These are obligations which arise from undertakings, promises, contracts, etc. that you have decided to make. Your obligation to be there at 2:00, because you promised someone that you would be there at 2:00, is a particular, voluntary obligation. The other class of particular obligations is non-voluntary. Such obligations arise from particular episodes in your life, but not from episodes (like promising) where you had the option to determine whether they would occur or not. An example of a particular, non-voluntary obligation is the obligation of gratitude owed by the child of loving, caring parents to those parents.

Now if I am right Locke has failed to show, and could not even have hoped to show, that the obligation to obey the state is a particular, voluntary obligation. But this leaves at least two other options, assuming that my list of kinds of obligation is exhaustive. The first is that the obligation to obey political authority might be a general obligation. It is a fundamental assumption of the contract tradition that the obligation to obey the state, if it exists at all, is a particular obligation. But it is not immediately obvious that this must be so.

Some unsatisfactory reasons for supposing that this obligation must be a particular obligation will now be mentioned. It may be said that if there is an obligation to obey the state, then it cannot be that all persons at all times have had it. For people may find themselves in a situation where there is no clearly established political authority: say, when they are emeshed in a civil war, or when they find themselves in a place where there has been a breakdown of civil authority. But this does not show that there cannot be a general obligation to obey political authority. For in the case of other general obligations people can be in circumstances where the obligation does not call for any particular action or restraint. For example, Robinson Crusoe's general obligation to respect the physical integrity of others did not require him to act in any particular way before Friday arrived. Similarly a general obligation to obey political authority may not always require one to act in some particular way.

It may be said that political obligation, if it exists, is particular in the sense that an individual owes this obligation to some particular political authority. For example, an Englishman, if he owes it, owes it to the Queen in Parliament. (This would imply that the obligation to obey the law when visiting a foreign country is different from the obligation to obey the law in one's own country.) Supposing this is true, it would not show that the obligation was particular; i.e. that it depended on the occurrence of some particular episode in a person's life. For the ground of an obligation can be general, while the obligation generated by it can be to a particular person. For example, respect for the physical integrity of all persons obliges you not to hit this person, who is making you very angry. Therefore it is still a possibility that a case for the authority of the state could be grounded on some suitable general obligation. Though I cannot, it is true, think what this general obligation might be.

Now to turn to the second option alluded to earlier. Political obligation might be a species of *non-voluntary* particular obligation. We believe that certain obligations arise for us as a result of the particular courses that our lives have taken, even if we could not have done anything to avoid our lives taking those courses. An example would be an obligation to help an elderly relative who had done us good when we were younger. This leads to the possibility that we might justify an obligation on the part of some person to obey some state on the basis of gratitude. It should be noted that this argument is *not* a contract argument, because it is not being supposed that persons who incur such obligations usually have a choice as to whether they will incur them.

As Locke does not attempt to use this kind of argument it is not appropriate to try to explore it fully here.[2] Briefly, there seem to me to be four difficulties in the way of accepting this as a ground for political obligation.

1. States claim universal authority over all those within their jurisdiction. But not all those within their jurisdiction would have had a history that was appropriate for generating political obligation. For example, some might have been brought up within the jurisdiction of another state, and have only recently come to this state.
2. For you to have an obligation of gratitude you must have received some benefit. Can all of those within the jurisdiction of a state be supposed to have benefited from the existence of that state? Have the homeless on the streets benefited? The

argument calls for an account of a minimally just state, but it seems unlikely that all of those within the jurisdiction of a state could be said to have benefited.

3. On this argument no one could be said to have an obligation unless there were a history of association between that state and that particular individual. In this regard, the gratitude argument fails to explain a 'quasi-obligation' which my approach could justify. Consider, for example, the position of a liberal, democratic German in Germany at the end of the Second World War. The occupying powers are attempting to set up a liberal democratic administration in West Germany. There would be no obligation to obey this new government on the basis of association, for what this person has been associated with has been the Third Reich, which is now no more. But it still could be reasonable to act *as if* the new liberal democratic government had authority, if the prospects for its being a decent government seemed good.

4. Normally, when it is conceded that an obligation of gratitude does exist, there is some flexibility in how that gratitude might be expressed. For example, it would be assumed that you have some choice in how you help an elderly relative, given that you acknowledge that you have an obligation of gratitude. But the state presumes to name what it shall take as an expression of gratitude – obedience.

Conclusion

The failure of Locke's argument suggests that the state, conceived of correctly, and operating in a satisfactory way, is merely a functional organization. The judgements we are to make of it, and upon which any habit of obedience is to be based, rest upon its performance in achieving certain desirable goals. So the failure of Locke's attempt to found political authority upon individual contractual consent is not without its benefits. It helps us to understand the correct way in which to conceive of our relationship to the state. This involves understanding that political authority, properly speaking, does not exist.

In its place we should consider what reasons we may have for acting *as if* the state had authority.

It is appropriate to conclude this part of the argument by considering one more way in which we can arrive at the same conclusion. To accept that a state had authority would be, in effect, to accept that it had moral authority. For to believe yourself to be under a political obligation is to believe yourself to have a moral obligation to do certain things in the political realm. Political obligations are a sub-set of moral obligations, just as parental obligations are a sub-set of moral obligations. If you think you have political obligations with respect to a certain political authority, then you think that you prima facie ought to do as it directs, setting aside the reasons arising from the threat of force, punishment, etc. with which the state may be able to provide you.

So to accept that a state has authority is to accept that you have a moral obligation to obey it. Now a moral obligation does not leave you with the autonomy to choose whether to act in accordance with that obligation or not. (A moral obligation may leave you with some discretion as to how and when, exactly, to fulfil it. You may be able to choose whether to repay today or tomorrow. But it does not leave you with the choice of *whether* you fulfil the obligation. You are not morally free. Of course you can fail to do what you are not morally free not to do.) Now if the argument recently given is correct, citizens, by contrast, *do* have the moral autonomy to decide whether it is reasonable to obey the state or not. Therefore the position in which they stand (even when they do decide to obey) is not the position one is in when one is subject to a moral obligation.

This perspective on the relationship between the citizen and the state has implications for contemporary debates about the 'transfer of sovereignty'. A current instance of this issue is provided by debates about the transfer of functions from the national governments within the European Union to central institutions. Those who complain about such transfers 'on principle' (i.e. without regard to what might be thought to be the advantages or disadvantages in the particular case) imagine that nation-states have authority in a way which is being denied by my argument. They imagine that some nation-states have an authority which can be established on the basis of past-regarding considerations. But the truth is that if certain activities can be controlled by central European Union institutions in a way that is functionally superior to national control, then there is no objection 'on principle', related to issues of political authority, which stands in the way of such transfers. The nation-state never had some species of 'better-grounded authority' than the European Union institutions will come to have (so long as they manage these activities in a functionally effective way).

There is one further consideration which might be brought in here. Suppose we have a system of government with a *de facto* near-monopoly of power for enforcing the law of nature. And suppose that what this state actually enforces is, in the great majority of cases, a plausible and reasonable interpretation of the law of nature. Now some of the citizens of this state, following the line of thought I have just pursued, may reflect as follows: 'This state enforces a view of what the law of nature requires which is, in its way, plausible and reasonable enough. Nevertheless, sometimes some of us take a different view of what the law of nature requires, and it has not been shown that the state has any *authority* to require us to accept its different view. So we will not take any notice of what the state requires in those cases where its interpretation does not correspond to ours.' The following response to such reflections would seem appropriate: 'Your attitude is likely to cause trouble. There are great advantages to everyone if only *one* view of what the law of nature requires is followed. So you owe it to the rest of us not to exercise your right, which we acknowledge you to have in view of the state's lack of authority, It would be very inconsiderate towards the rest of us (who are nearly always prepared to put up with the state's interpretation of the law of nature) to insist on exercising your right not to accept it.'

It is plausible that one may enjoy a right, but also be subject to some moral consideration telling against exercising that right in a certain way, or in certain circumstances. For example, you have a right not to lend your ladder to your neighbour (as it is your ladder). But if your neighbour needs it to get her child out of danger, then you (morally) ought not to exercise your right not to lend it. I would accept that there is this argument for following the interpretation of the law of nature proposed by the state (given that the interpretation

55

is reasonable). It is an important consequentialist argument for following it, but it does not affect the position that the state, strictly speaking, lacks authority.

Locke fails to show how a state can come to have legitimate authority by way of a social contract. But probably there is no way in which it could be shown that a state has authority, strictly speaking. Often in philosophy arguments fail to establish their intended conclusions, but nevertheless are far from valueless. Locke's analysis reveals important insights into the structure of the state and the nature of political power. It also shows us that we were trying to do the wrong thing in seeking an argument for the authority of the state. All we need are reasonable grounds for a disposition to comply with the requirements of a (decent) state.

Chapter 3

Rebellion

Introduction: what is revolution?

We now turn to consider Locke's case for claiming that rebellion can be justifiable. In the previous chapter it has been argued that Locke's analysis of the state illuminates the nature of political authority, but that ultimately it is not successful, in that it does not justify political authority. In this chapter we shall see that Locke's case for rebellion is more directly successful, and indeed much of it is still quite credible to us.

I have already said that Locke's main point in writing the *Second Treatise* was to justify rebellion. For Locke to claim that there was a way in which a state could come to have genuine authority was hardly extraordinary to his contemporaries. What was extraordinary was to argue that the very grounds for holding that a state had legitimate authority (given that it satisfied certain

conditions) were also grounds for rebellion (if it failed to satisfy those conditions). The Court Party (or Tories) claimed that if you sought to justify rebellion you would subvert the basis of legitimate government. Locke said, on the contrary, that the true basis of legitimate government also served, in the appropriate circumstances, to provide the justification of rebellion.

Why is the theory of rebellion comparatively neglected in discussions of Locke's political philosophy, while so much more attention is given to the theory of political obligation, and to his discussion of private property? After all, no commentator, so far as I am aware, regards these latter parts of Locke's work as successful in establishing the conclusions intended. Two speculations come to mind by way of an answer. Locke is intending to justify all-out armed rebellion against those who claim to be the government. Such episodes have not much been a part of the political life of most Anglo-Saxon states. The United States has not experienced such events since the end of the Civil War, and Britain has not had any such episodes of note since Locke's own day. So it may seem that Locke's theory is rather remote from Anglo-Saxon political life, in a way that it would not seem to be remote from, say, Russian political life.

What has been a more regular part of Anglo-Saxon political life is civil disobedience. The deliberate breaking of the law in order to further a cause believed to be just has been part of the United States civil rights movement, the anti-Vietnam war protests, the British suffragette movement and the more recent protests against the English poll tax. In so far as anti-legal or extra-legal political action has been considered in Anglo-Saxon political theory it has tended to be civil disobedience rather revolution. In *A Theory of Justice* Rawls discusses civil disobedience (Rawls 1972, Chapter VI), but the issue of revolution is never raised, and the situation where a state is so unjust as to provide grounds for all-out revolution is not considered. Locke is not, however, considering the more genteel issue of civil disobedience. For though civil disobedience involves law-breaking, it is not seriously intended to disrupt the processes of government or to overturn the state. Locke is discussing all-out armed revolution. So far as civil disobedience is concerned, he probably would have condemned it so long as the government remained legitimate.

Another reason for the relative neglect of Locke's theory of rebellion may be the ideological influence of the contemporary British ruling class. The nationalist right, at least, is disposed to distance itself with a show of disdain from some of the political traditions of the continent, and to make exaggerated claims about the stability and continuity of British political life. It does not fit entirely comfortably with this view to recognize that one of greatest English political thinkers was in theory and in practice a committed revolutionary.

What is a political revolution? A revolution involves two main areas of change: in those who govern, and in the institutional structures according to which political processes occur. In a revolution there will be a change in the persons who wield effective political power which is not legitimate by reference to the existing political practices and institutions of that political community. This change will occur first, but normally there also will be formal changes in the political institutions some time later. These will have been brought about by processes not themselves legitimate in terms of the old political forms. However, there may be some attempt on the part of the revolutionaries to make out that the changes are legitimate in terms of the traditional political processes. This happened in the case of the overthrow of James II and his replacement by William and Mary. Examples which satisfy this general account of revolution are the English Revolution of the 1640s, the French Revolution of 1789 and the Bolshevik Revolution of 1917.

The question of whether changes have occurred according to the established institutions of a political community is crucial for deciding whether there has been a revolution. A change in the class, nationality or religion of those groups who exercise political power might be very striking, and indeed might often be referred to as a 'revolution', without really being one in the sense which concerns us here. For example, the coming to power of Attlee's administration in Britain in 1945 might be called a 'revolution' in this sense, considering the difference in the social origin of at least some of the people who held power, as compared with what had been usual before in British political life. But that was not a revolution in the sense which concerns us here, for that administration was elected by the normal constitutional processes of the political community. Analogous things may be said about the policies the Attlee administration introduced. Again, changes in the constitutional processes themselves, though they might be very considerable, would not be 'revolutionary' in the way intended here if they were brought about by procedures all of which were legitimate in terms of existing constitutional practice. Suppose a radical British administration, elected in the present way, were to introduce a modern electoral system for the House of Commons, abolish the House of Lords and the monarchy, and introduce a written constitution. No doubt this would be called a 'revolution' in British political life, but if each step in this process were legitimate in terms of the then political practice of the country (if, for example, the abolition of the monarchy were passed by both Houses of Parliament and received the Royal Assent), then this would not be a 'revolution' in the sense which concerns us here.

Locke's conditions for justifiable rebellion

An account of Locke's theory of justifiable rebellion may be developed on the basis of his 'core' theory of the state, as outlined in the last chapter. Suppose we start out with a situation in which, according to Locke, a government rules with right, and its citizens have an obligation to obey. What alterations in the situation would have to take place in order for the government to cease to be legitimate, and for it to be morally permissible for the people to attempt to resist it, by force if necessary?

First we should remind ourselves of what, in Lockean terms, a rebellion would be. A legitimate government (i.e. a set of persons holding political power with right) will satisfy two conditions. The first is that they will be the appropriate persons to hold the political offices in question by reference to the constitution of that political society. For example, they will have been elected by the constitutionally prescribed processes. The second is that the body of citizens (in Locke, the 'community') continue to place their trust in that constitutional form. Without that trust the constitutional form will lack legitimacy for that political community. The scene for a rebellion is set, therefore, when a majority of the community have withdrawn their trust, thereby leaving the constitution, and the people empowered under it, without legitimacy. If those who have held political power do not in those circumstances depart, but instead try to hang on to power by force, a rebellion or revolution comes about. Strictly speaking, as Locke insists, it is not the people who rebel against the government, because those who formerly had authority *are* no longer the people's government. Rather, it is the former governors who rebel against the people, in that they attempt to retain by force power which is no longer rightfully theirs (II.226–8).

This can be thought of as the basic case of rebellion for Locke. An illustration would be the stance of the disaffected colonists in the American colonies towards the British colonial governors in the 1770s. They sought to throw off one constitutional form of government and to replace it with another. But in the case of Locke's disaffection with Charles II and James II it seems not so much that Locke was dissatisfied with the existing British constitution as with the (allegedly unconstitutional) actions of those monarchs. The official Whig view was that the replacement of James II by William and Mary took place within the existing constitution. Evidence of this ambiguity in Locke is to be found in the opening of II.226, where he is arguing that it is the illegitimate government, rather than the people, who rebel. Locke says

> this doctrine of a power in the people of providing for their safety anew by a new legislative, when their legislators have acted contrary to their trust by invading their property, is the best fence against rebellion, and the probablest means to hinder it.

The reference of 'by a new legislative' is ambiguous as between 'by a newly elected (and presumably largely different) group of persons elected under the existing constitution' and 'by a newly elected (and presumably largely different) group of persons elected under a *new* constitution to which the people have entrusted their power anew'. Nothing in these three sections (i.e. II.226–8) entirely clarifies Locke's position, and the ambiguity is perhaps intentional. For Locke did not know at the time of writing whether the situation he sought to remedy could be dealt with (as it eventually was) by having a Protestant monarch prepared to act within a parliamentary constitution, or whether it would prove necessary to make a radical change to the constitution.

A number of general grounds for justifiable rebellion can be discerned in Locke. To begin with I will simply set them out.

A. Government fails to enforce the law of nature

A government provides grounds for rebellion if it fails to enforce the law of nature. Such a failure may take one of two forms.

1. The government may effectively enforce policies directly contrary to the law of nature. An example would be the genocidal policies of the Nazi government of Germany in the 1940s. It follows from Locke's theory of the state, as sketched out in the last chapter, that it must be illegitimate for a government to act in this way. The only power a community can entrust to a government is the executive power of the law of nature of all of its members. That power is, by definition, a power only to enforce the law of nature (II.135). No government could have the power to act in an arbitrary and tyrannical way, for no person in the state of nature had the right to act in such a way, and all the power a government has must originally come from the people. Locke is aware that governments will perpetrate minor violations of the law of nature, due to the corruption of officials and the imperfect operation of the state's institutions. An example would be the imprisonment of the wrong person. But he does not suggest that grounds for rebellion are supplied every time there is such a mistake. As Locke says in II.225, 'revolutions happen not upon every little mismanagement in public affairs'.

2. Less commonly, the failure to enforce the law of nature may be a matter of continuously ineffectual attempts to do so, rather than a matter of perverse intention (II.219).

Both grounds for rebellion may in principle arise under any form of government; under oligarchies and democracies, as well as under monarchies (II.201).

B. Government fails to further the common good

A government provides grounds for rebellion if it acts other than to further the public or common good (II.131). At II.3 Locke defines political power as a right of making laws only for the public good. It is not entirely clear what Locke has in mind when he refers to the common or public good. One possibility is that to govern for the common good is to govern in such a way as to effectively enforce the law of nature: that is, to remedy the 'inconveniencies' of the state of nature, as was intended by those who made the original compact. This view is suggested by a passage at II.131:

> the power of the society, or legislative constituted by them, can never be supposed to extend further than the common good; but is obliged to secure everyone's property by providing against those three defects above-mentioned that made the state of nature so unsafe and uneasy

If the government furthers the common good in this sense, then it effectively enforces everyone's rights. Locke puts the point by saying that it preserves their *properties* (II.94, 124, 139, 171), for by a person's 'property' in this context Locke means her life, liberty and estate (II.87, 123, 173); that is, all that over which she has rights. Locke is here making use of an extended meaning of the term 'property'. What he says in no way implies that the only or main purpose of government is to defend people's rights to their material possessions.

So far this new condition takes us no further than the ground already covered in (A). There is, however, one further idea which is contained in Locke's conception of the public good: the preservation and safety of the whole society. The enforcement of the law of nature will, of course, tend to preserve the members of the society, but Locke seems to think that there may be things beyond this which a government will have to do for the sake of preservation. An example is provided by Locke's illustration of the legitimate exercise of 'prerogative': pulling down houses in the path of an urban fire in an attempt to stop the fire spreading (II.160). This is not simply enforcing the law of nature. On the contrary, on the face of it, it is violating it, as it is destroying people's property. But it is defensible in terms of the common or public good. The right of government to do this is provided for by a power additional to the executive power of the law of nature, a power which is also transferred to the community at the time of the original compact. (Mention of this additional power was omitted from the exposition in the previous chapter because of the complications it would have introduced.) It is the power of an individual in the state of nature 'to do whatsoever he thinks fit for the preservation of himself and others within the permission of the law of nature' (II.128). It is this aspect of Locke's conception of the public good which is emphasized in II.135. 'Their power, in the utmost bounds of it, is limited to the public good of the society. It is a power that hath no other end but preservation.'

It will be clear, incidentally, that Locke is a long way from 'minimal statism'. Government has an obligation to further the common good in ways additional to the enforcement of the law of nature.

C. *Government loses trust*

The government exercises the executive power of the law of nature on trust from the majority of the community (II.149). If the government loses the attitudinal consent of the majority, it loses its legitimacy. Should a government nevertheless continue to try to exercise power over its citizens, they have the right to resist, by force if necessary. Cases in the recent past where this condition for rebellion would have been satisfied would be Romania and the former East Germany.

It is an implication of this condition that a government loses its legitimacy if it attempts to hand over its power to some other authority; for example, to a foreign government. As the people entrusted their power to a specific authority, that authority has no right to place the power it has received in any other hands unless it has the consent of the people. The power does not belong to the government but to the people, and it is not for the government to dispose of it in any way that it pleases (II.217). (Here Locke particularly had in mind his concern that Charles II would allow, indeed encourage, the British government to come under the control of Louis XIV.) Similarly the usurpation of the power of a legitimate government (for example, by a successful coup) would provide grounds for resistance to the usurpers, for the people have not consented to the usurpers having that power (II.197, 198, 199). It is being assumed here, of course, that the coup is being mounted by a minority, and is lacking the support of the majority of the people.

D. Government fails to act within the bounds of positive law

Finally, Locke requires that a government must act within the bounds of the established positive law and the existing constitutional practice of the political community in question (II.136, 200, 202). The constitutions of legitimate political authorities do not have to be identical in every respect. For example, some might have an oligarchic system, while others have a democratic one (II.132). Only similarities in certain respects are required: for example, that they all respect natural law. And even here Locke would appear to allow the exception of prerogative, as we have just seen. It might be argued, though, that Locke regarded the exercise of prerogative as in effect allowed by constitutional practice. A particular and pressing case of the executive not conforming to positive law was the attempts of Charles II to prevent Parliament from meeting. Locke also thought that this requirement of conformity to positive law ruled out the executive taking property without the authorization of Parliament (II.138–40).

How are Locke's conditions to be applied?

This completes the list of basic circumstances in which Locke thinks that rebellion is justifiable. Other circumstances are mentioned, but these would seem to derive from (D), together with what Locke believed British constitutional practice required. In the next part of the discussion I want to draw attention to the difference between condition (C), the attitudinal consent requirement, and the others. The others make no essential reference to the *attitudes* of the citizens. For example, if natural law is violated this is so whatever anyone believes. However, (C) depends on the attitude towards the government taken up by the majority of the citizens. Two situations in which this difference stands out will be important in the subsequent discussion.

1. A government may fail to live up to the requirement that it enforce the law of nature because, for example, it violates the natural rights of some of its citizens. Nevertheless it may continue to enjoy the attitudinal consent of the majority to the continuance of the trust. Possibly the situation at some times in Nazi Germany would have provided an illustration of this; though it is very difficult to say, of course, to what extent that government would have enjoyed uncoerced majority support.

2. Another possibility is that a government should lose the consent of the majority to the continuance of the trust, even though the government *has* enforced the law of nature and promoted the common good. A government could become unpopular with the majority because of its religious, racial or class composition, even though it supplied no grounds for rebellion under (A), (B) or (D).

Locke does not much consider the possibility that grounds for rebellion may be supplied under (A), (B) or (D), but not under (C); or that grounds may be supplied under (C), but not under (A), (B) or (D). With one exception, to be discussed shortly, Locke appears to believe that these circumstances for rebellion will go in harness. If a government fails to enforce the law of nature or to promote the common good, it will lose the consent of the majority. If it loses the consent of the majority this will be because it failed under one or more of (A), (B) or (D).

Why did Locke not give greater attention to this difficulty in his theory? My speculation is that he assumes that most people are 'rational' (in the sense in which Locke would understand that term in this context, i.e. 'practically rational') when giving or withholding their attitudinal consent. In II.163 he makes reference to 'a society of rational creatures'. Probably he thought that most people would cease to give their consent if they became aware of significant failures of the government to enforce the law of nature. Nor would most people withdraw their consent for 'frivolous' reasons: that is, reasons having nothing to do with the law of nature or the common good. Locke's assumption is open to criticism, of course, from the tradition of political theorizing which emphasizes the importance of the so-called 'non-rational' in politics: that is, the influence of locality, custom, nationality, and ethnic and religious affiliation as against 'rational' considerations. In addition, Locke could not have envisaged the capacity of the modern totalitarian state to conceal from its citizens many of the terrible things going on, because no state at his time had the modern capacity to control the means of communication.

Nevertheless it does seem appropriate to confront Locke with this question: what if a government fails to enforce the law of nature but enjoys the consent of the majority; or enforces the law of nature but fails to enjoy the consent of the majority? My view is that when pressed Locke would say that the consent condition (C) has priority over the other three. Even if it would appear that one or more of (A), (B) and (D) applied, this would not allow us to say that rebellion is justified unless (C) also applied. Locke's thinking behind this is possibly along the following lines. With respect to conditions (A), (B) and (D) there is, characteristically, controversy over how they apply in particular situations. It cannot be expected that everyone will agree on their application, but it is crucial to the legitimacy of government that a common view be reached. So we need a decision-making process. But what could it be? Not the processes of government themselves, for it is their legitimacy that is being called into question. If the government had to judge on its own legitimacy, no doubt it would judge favourably. So this way of resolving matters would *de facto* rule out any justifiable rebellions. But neither is it satisfactory to appeal to the conscience of the individual citizen. For if she were allowed to disobey the government whenever she was prepared to claim that it was against her conscience to obey, we would, in effect, release her from a moral obligation to obey any law she did not like. Locke notes this at II.97. Therefore the appropriate decision-making process would seem to be one which involves the majority of the community. This very neatly solves the problem posed by the dismissal of the other two proposals.

The term 'community', in the context of Locke's political theory, has a specific meaning, as was noted in the previous chapter (see the section entitled 'The Formation of the Community').

The 'community' consists of all those persons who have, by compact, incorporated themselves on the basis of surrendering their executive powers of the law of nature to the control of the group. The communal power is in the hands of the community until it is entrusted to a form of government of their choosing. It reverts to the control of the community if it is decided that that trust should be ended.

It is interesting to note, in this respect, how Locke differs from Hobbes. Hobbes denied that there was any right of rebellion against the sovereign (Hobbes 1968, 229: *Leviathan*, Part II, Chapter 18), though he did allow that an individual may resist a sovereign who intends to kill her (Hobbes 1968, 269: *Leviathan*, Part II, Chapter 21). Also, Hobbes made no room for any form of political association other than that of the commonwealth with a sovereign power. Locke's claim that rebellion sometimes can be justifiable requires the introduction of the notion of the 'community'. This idea avoids the individual having so strong a right of conscience as to destroy any moral claim to obedience on the part of the state, but it also avoids allowing the state to judge in its own case without any right of appeal on the part of the citizen.

Substantial evidence for this interpretation is provided by a passage at II.230.

> Nor let anyone say that mischief can arise from hence as often as it shall please a busy head, or turbulent spirit, to desire the alteration of the government. 'Tis true, such men may stir whenever they please, but it will be only to their own just ruin and perdition. For till the mischief be grown general, and the ill designs of the rulers become visible, or their attempts sensible to the greater part, the people, who are more disposed to suffer than right themselves by resistance, are not apt to stir. The examples of particular injustice, or oppression of here and there an unfortunate man, moves them not. But if they universally have a persuasion, grounded upon manifest evidence, that designs are carrying on against their liberties, and the general course and tendency of things cannot but give them strong suspicions of the evil intentions of their governors, who is to be blamed for it?

Further evidence for such an interpretation is to be found at
II.240.

> Who shall be judge whether the prince or legislative act contrary
> to their trust? . . . To this I reply: The people shall be judge.
> For who shall be judge whether his trustee or deputy acts well,
> and according to the trust reposed in him, but he who deputes
> him, and must, by having deputed him, have still a power to
> discard him when he fails in his trust?

The most plausible interpretation of Locke on this point is, therefore,
that if a government fails under one or more of the conditions (A),
(B) or (D), but does *not* fail under the consent condition (C), then the
government remains legitimate. Locke is somewhat less of an indi-
vidualist than is often supposed. In making the original compact an
individual gives up any unilateral right of resistance to government, and accepts that this right now lies with the majority of the
community.

Locke's theory is less individualistic than is usually supposed
in a further respect. So far no distinction has been made between the
view that resistance to government is permissible, though not obligatory, and the stronger view that resistance is obligatory. For Locke it
would seem that when the majority withdraws its consent, the existing
government becomes illegitimate. Everyone is then bound by the original compact to resist if the government continues to try to exercise
power: those who were not part of the majority as well as those who
were. Not only may you not resist if the majority has not withdrawn
its trust, but you are bound *to* resist if the majority *has* withdrawn its
trust. The account of Locke's position proposed here is based on what
may be inferred from what Locke does say. To my knowledge Locke
does not expressly state such a view.

While the position outlined is the one I think it is most reasonable to attribute to Locke, it must be allowed that not everything in
the text supports it. One piece of apparent counter-evidence is to be
found at II.168.

> And where the body of the people, *or any single man*, is
> deprived of their right, or is under the exercise of a power

> without right, and have no appeal on earth, there they have a liberty to appeal to heaven whenever they judge the cause of sufficient moment. (Italics added.)

This appears to suggest that an individual may have a right of unilateral resistance. This intimation is not confirmed, however, if we read on to the end of the section, which re-affirms the majoritarian criterion.

> Nor let anyone think this lays a perpetual foundation for disorder: for this operates not, till the inconvenience is so great that the majority feel it, and are weary of it, and find a necessity to have it amended.

Apparently Locke's meaning is that the deprivation of the rights of a particular person may be a sufficient *occasion* for the majority to withdraw its consent, but no one has a *right* to resist unless this single instance has persuaded the majority to withdraw its consent.

A passage which it is less easy to reconcile with the interpretation offered occurs at II.208:

> if the unlawful acts done by the magistrate be maintained (by the power he has got) and the remedy which is due by law be by the same power obstructed, yet the right of resisting, even in such manifest acts of tyranny, will not suddenly, or on slight occasions, disturb the government. For if it reach no further than some private men's cases, though they have a right to defend themselves, and to recover by force what by unlawful force is taken from them, yet the right to do so will not easily engage them in a contest wherein they are sure to perish; it being as impossible for one or a few oppressed men to disturb the government, where the body of the people do not think themselves concerned in it, as for a raving madman or heady malcontent to overturn a well-settled state.

Here Locke appears to be saying quite clearly that there *is* a right of forceful resistance on the part of those to whom due process of law is denied, but that this right of resisting will not in fact lead to rebellion, for if most people are unconcerned about the case, resistance by a few will be futile. It is strange that Locke should allow both that an individual has a right to resist the magistrate *and* that it is quite satisfactory that nothing should be done about enforcing that right. This is especially so if we recall a passgage at II.7 where Locke says that a law is vain if there is no one who has the power to execute it. Locke's position would be made consistent if it were said that the individuals in such a case do not have a right of resistance until the majority are moved by their cause. Of course you would be stupid to resist if there were only a few of you. But the issue is one about what you have a *right* to do. Equally it could be stupid for the majority to resist, if the government has all the tanks, but that does not affect what they have a right to do.

How plauslble is Locke's position on rebellion?

As a preliminary to considering how plausible Locke's position is from a contemporary point of view, it is appropriate to review its implications in a number of different situations.

1. Locke's position sanctions resistance (including forceful resistance by a substantial part of the community) when the majority has withdrawn its trust. Locke's position would seem to imply, therefore, that some of the great revolutions, such as the English of the 1640s and the French of 1789, were justifiable. I hesitate to add the American War of Independence, however, for this reason: Locke's case for justifiable rebellion presupposes that the composition of a particular political *community* is not in dispute. But if, as in the American War of Independence, the issue is (in Lockean terms) whether there is one or two independent political communities, no determinate answer may be possible on whether resistance is justifiable.

   Locke always assumes that *who* are members of the political community is not in question. According to Locke this has already been decided by considering which individuals choose to incorporate themselves into a particular body politic. Therefore Locke's theory of justifiable rebellion can give no account of the situation where a group is seeking national autonomy, and the issue is 'How many political communities are there to be?' In such a case the established government well may have a plausible case to the effect that they enjoy the consent of the majority of those they consider to be the community; that is, the whole of the nation-state of which they are the government. The rebels also may be able to argue plausibly that in what they consider to be the community they are the majority, and that they do not consent. (Consider, for example, the advocates of Scottish independence and the position of those who continue to advocate the union of Great Britain.) Locke's theory does not seem to be applicable to this kind of situation. This seriously restricts its comprehensiveness as a theory of justifiable rebellion.

2. Locke's position would permit neither forceful nor non-violent resistance by a minority if the majority wishes to continue its trust. Two examples are of interest here. It is questionable whether Locke's position would permit forcible, or even non-violent, resistance to a government violating the rights of some of its citizens if the majority were not moved to withdraw its trust. And it is doubtful whether Locke's position would allow non-violent resistance by a minority when this was intended as an appeal to the majority to rectify injustice. That is to say, Locke's positon would not appear to allow for the kind of civil disobedience which Rawls considers to be permissible (Rawls 1972, 371–7). However, consideration of such cases is complicated by the fact that Locke does not consider resistance except in the context of an intention to precipitate the overthrow of government.

The problem with Locke's position on revolution from our perspective is not that it may be thought to sanction too much resistance, but that it may be thought to sanction too little. If a minority is having its rights systematically violated by the government, it would seem that this minority does not have a right to resist, so long as the majority do not withdraw their trust from the government. The main worry of a modern audience about Locke's theory of justifiable rebellion is the importance it gives to the majority of the community as against the conscience of the individual. True, the conscience of the individual counts, in that the majority opinion will be formed from the opinions of the individuals in the community. But no individual has the right to resist unilaterally if the majority of the community has not withdrawn its trust. This leads us to consider whether Locke has a strong enough case, in terms of his own theory, for giving such decisive importance to the will of the majority.

Locke's argument for his position begins with your consenting (contractually) to the original compact to transfer your executive power of the law of nature to the community. In doing this you must be understood to bind yourself to the decision of the majority of the community on where the power is to be entrusted. Why should you be understood as having consented to this? The end reasonable persons have in surrendering their executive power of the law of nature is remedying the 'inconveniencies' of the state of nature. A rational person is committed to anything necessary for this end. Now the 'inconveniencies' of the state of nature can be remedied only if the body politic acts with one will. You expect to be better off than in the state of nature if you are subject to a common interpretation and enforcement of the law of nature. But you would have been better off to have retained your executive power of the law of nature if you could not anticipate that there would be a common power to enforce your natural rights. Now if there is to be a common power there must be agreeement on where the collectivized executive power of the law of nature is to be placed. Any other stand would be self-defeating, given the intention you had in quitting the state of nature. Therefore any reasonable person must accept a majoritarian decision procedure (II.97–9).

Locke's argument is weak. It establishes no more than that the procedure for entrusting the community's executive power of the law of nature should not be unanimity, for that procedure is very unlikely to result in a decision. But there is no reason why Locke's own majoritarian principle should result in a decision in all circumstances. There could be, for example, roughly equal factions for entrusting power to a democracy, an oligarchy and a monarchy, with no faction prepared to compromise sufficiently to allow a majority to form.

This objection could have been avoided if Locke had said that a member of the community is obliged to accept the view about where the executive power of the law of nature is to be placed which has *most* support. This support might be less than a majority. Under this proposal a decision would be reached in nearly all circumstances, but it would make Locke's theory of justifiable rebellion paradoxical. In some circumstances Locke would then have to say that a government is legitimate, because it is favoured by more members of the community than any alternative, and that it is not legitimate, because the majority do not consent to entrusting power to it. To be consistent the theory of rebellion would have to be altered so as to make rebellion permissible only if there is some alternative to the present form of government which would have the support of more members of the community than the present one.

This stipulation would, however, unacceptably reduce the number of circumstances in which it would be possible to justify revolution. In some situations where there is a profoundly unpopular government, there is an opposition party waiting to inherit its power. For example, when Marcos was deposed in the Phillipines the established opposition party of Mrs Core Aquino was ready to assume power. But often there is no properly established party to provide an alternative, as in the case of the French Revolution of 1789. It is to be expected that this will happen often in a revolutionary situation, especially when a cause of the revolution has been the denial of political rights, as in the case of the revolutions in Eastern Europe at the end of the 1980s. The denial of political rights and the related political repression will have been intended to make it difficult for opposition parties to form. It will also have made it difficult for people to indicate their support for opposition parties. So the lack of a clear alternative to a deposed government is likely to be a quite common situation after a successful revolution.

Another possibility would be for Locke to allow that in some circumstances a community may be so badly divided that it cannot reach a majority decision on where power is to be entrusted. He could then say that *if* a majority can form, you are bound to accept its decision (it being allowed that there may be circumstances in which a majority cannot be formed). But it is now unclear why this criterion should be regarded as the one that has to be accepted. We are balancing the claims of attitudinal consent against the urgency of reaching a decision about where power is to be entrusted. It also matters to Locke that an effective common decision-making process for the society should be established as soon as possible. If one gave greater weight to the urgency of a decision being reached, one might opt for the view that a person is bound by the opinion which simply has most support. If one gave less weight to that, one might insist on attitudinal consent by more than a majority. Is there any criterion one is rationally bound to accept?

This is not to suggest that Locke's difficulty at this point is to be regarded as a mere internal inadequacy of his theory. Locke is trying to solve a genuine and difficult problem, the existence of which is not the creation of his theory. On the one hand, we may be reluctant to allow that before any form of forceful resistance to government by an individual is morally permissible, the majority must have withdrawn its attitudinal consent. What, for example, if the government is violating the natural rights of some of its citizens on a significant scale, and yet the majority does not withdraw its consent? But if we reject Locke's criterion, what are we to put in its place? Are we to say that the moral conscience of the individual is to be freed from *any* constraint imposed by the opinions of his or her fellow citizens? If anyone is of the sincere opinion that the government is failing to carry out its trust (in that it is violating the natural rights of some of its citizens), is it then morally permissible for that person to resist? (Of course it may be stupid to attempt to resist by force if few are on your side, but this is not the point here.) This alternative may well strike us as unsatisfactory also. It does not acknowledge that citizens are members of a body politic (the 'community'). It gives them no less freedom of action than if they were still in the state of nature. Locke points this out effectively in II.97.

> And thus every man, by consenting with others to make one body politic under one government, puts himself under an obligation to everyone of that society to submit to the determination of the majority, and to be concluded by it; or else this original compact, whereby he with others incorporates into one society, would signify nothing, and be no compact, if he be left free, and under no other ties, than he was in before, in the state of

nature. For what appearance would there be of any compact? What new engagement if he were no further tied by any decrees of the society than he himself thought fit and did actually consent to?

What is the point of having a state if it is not to serve as a way of making collective decisions? If any of us could ignore the decision procedures of the state at will, this would subvert these processes as our common decision procedures.

Of course you might not accept the idea that you *are* bound to your fellow citizens by some kind of moral relationship. You might think that there is really no contract, express or tacit; nor any other basis on which it could be claimed that a moral relationship exists between the citizens of a state. Indeed the discussion in Chapter 2 suggested that this is the correct position. In other words, you might say that the only tie between you and your fellow citizens, *qua* fellow citizen, is that the state deems you to be within its territories and to be subject to its jurisdiction. This is not necessarily a moral tie. Of course you might wish to say that there are non-contractual *moral* ties between the citizens. But these are not ties that exist *qua citizen*. They are ties that exist *qua human being*. However, what if you do believe that you are connected with your fellow citizens by a relationship that has a moral foundation? Then you could hardly affirm consistently that you are always at liberty from a moral point of view to ignore what your fellow citizens think, if you should happen to be of a different opinion.

There is a somewhat different way of looking at the situation which takes account of the point just made. It may be allowed that we are not in the state because we have taken part in some process of contractual consent. We simply find that we have landed up with a number of other people in some particular state, rather in the way in which we simply land up with a number of other people on an aeroplane. (Though in that case we have at least chosen to fly.) Even so, it may be argued, in the case of the state we find that there are these procedures, which customarily are used to decide matters. Do we not owe an obligation to our fellow citizens not to inconvenience them by ignoring the established decision procedure? Perhaps this is a plausible position to take if you are prepared to accept that the decision-making process is, from the moral point of view, at least tolerable. But what if in your view it is intolerable? (For example, it makes no provision for attempting to find out what is the view of God, and this you regard as blasphemous.) It is not clear that you have to accept the view of most of your fellow citizens about whether it is tolerable, unless you suppose that somehow you are already committed in turn to *that* decision-making process.

One further approach might be tried for dealing with this question. It may be argued that if persons consider themselves to be part of some organization, no matter what its specific character, then necessarily they will have to accept that their freedom of action will be constrained in ways in which it would not have been had they not been members of that organization. But this will not get us to the required conclusion. For even if persons do regard themselves as part of the organization, it does not follow that the constraints the organization imposes are the ones that it is necessary for any organization to impose. (For example, the organization might in fact impose restrictions on freedom of speech.) While it is plausible that membership of any organization necessarily involves the acceptance of some constraints, it does not follow that the acceptance of any particular set of constraints is necessary. And in any case the argument begs the question. For it to have any force a person would have to accept that he *is* a member of the organization in question. But an anarchist, for example, who is regarded by the state as a citizen, would not accept that (in moral reality) he is a member of that organization. He would say that from his point of view he has been arbitrarily deemed to be so.

Rebellion and the fundamental law of nature

So far we have discussed Locke's view that resistance by the individual is not permissible unless the majority of the community has withdrawn its attitudinal consent from the existing form of government. We have not yet considered another implication of Locke's theory of rebellion: that rebellion always *is* justifiable if the majority *does* withdraw its consent. This doctrine strikes a modern audience as intuitively plausible. If it appears that a government (a form of government, that is to say) has clearly lost the consent of the majority, as is true, for example, of the military government of Burma at the time of writing (1994), most would agree that there is no moral objection to resistance: certainly not to non-violent resistance, and perhaps not to violent resistance either. Does Locke's theory of justifiable rebellion give us sound reasons for this belief?

Locke's principal ground for his position is that the power government exercises is held on trust from the majority of the community (II.136 and II.149). If that is so: if, in other words, the community is the 'owner' of the power government exercises, then it must be that the community has the right to recover it.

> Who shall be judge whether the prince or legislative act contrary to their trust? . . . To this I reply: The people shall be judge. For who shall be judge whether his trustee or deputy acts well, and according to the trust reposed in him, but he who deputes him, and must, by having deputed him, have still a power to discard him when he fails in his trust? (II.240)

Presumably Locke does not think that the majority should have a right to recover their powers on a mere whim, say, because they happen to have taken a dislike to their form of government. They must have the genuine belief that the trust they placed in their system of government, that it would exercise the executive power of the law of nature on their behalf for the common good, has been abused.

But does this really show that political power *is* held on trust? Or is that contention an arbitrary claim relative to the rest of his theory? Locke argues that it will not do to have a double contract theory; i.e. a contract between individuals to incorporate themselves into a civil society, followed by a contract between the incorporated persons as a group and a prospective governmental body. For in that case, Locke asks, who would have the right to decide if there were a dispute between the governors and the people about whether the terms of their contract were being adhered to? But that leaves open two possibilities. One is that the people ultimately have the right to decide. The other is that the government ultimately has the right to decide. Why should it not be the latter? That is the option Hobbes took when considering the same issue. Locke needs an additional argument to show why it should be the people who decide.

This additional argument brings in a quite new kind of consideration. Locke's argument for regarding the relationship between the community and the government as one of trust depends on his idea of a fundamental law of nature. 'The fundamental law of nature being that all, as much as may be, should be preserved' (II.183. See also II.7, 16, 134, 149, 159). As mentioned earlier, Locke regarded more particular natural laws and natural rights as derived from the fundamental law of nature. Without going into the precise sense in which he regarded them as derivative, we can say, roughly speaking, that nothing can be a natural law or a natural right unless it is necessary to postulate it from the point of view of the fundamental law of nature, in conjunction with obvious facts. Thus, to take an earlier example, a person must have a natural right of access to the earth and its fruits. To suppose otherwise would be contrary to the fundamental law of nature, as it would deny a person the opportunity to preserve herself. Locke constructs an argument from the fundamental law of nature that is of relevance to the present case. Governments exercise great powers, which can and often have been used not to ensure the people's preservation, but to destroy some of them. By the fundamental law of nature, it could not be that the people lack the right to resist their own destruction. Therefore they must have a right to resist a government and recover the power it exercises over them. This is Locke's most plausible reason for insisting that the community must have a right of forceable resistance. It is reasonable that this right should be secured by regarding the power that a government exercises as entrusted to it by the people, who have a right to recover it at will. It is a reason Locke cites several times, in II.23, 149, 168 and 229.

Locke has here a good reason why the people should be regarded as having the right to rebel if a majority of them cease to consent to the government. It lays the basis for a moral defence of the right of the people to save themselves, if faced by regimes such as those of Stalin and Pol Pot. However there is another side to this argument. Locke believes, as has been said before, that the desirability of (legitimate) political order can be derived from the fundamental law of nature. Political society is more conducive to the preservation of man than the state of nature. So if, after a revolution, there is no clear alternative group who can hold power, and an interregnum or civil war follows, as in Russia after October 1917, this state of affairs, too, is undesirable from the point of view of the fundamental law of nature. So it is difficult to see how the relationship to the fundamental law of nature can be a decisive consideration, unless specific calculations about particular situations are made. In some cases, where the existing political authority is a notorious violator of its citizens' natural rights, and where there is a decent alternative grouping available to hold political power, it is obvious that it would be better from the point of view of the fundamental law of nature that a revolution should take place. (Though even in this case there would need to be some assurance that the revolution was likely to be successful without excessive suffering.) But where the existing holders of political power are not such bad violators of natural rights (though nevertheless clear enough violators of the trust that has been placed in them), and where it is very uncertain what the alternative would turn out to be like, it may be that a protracted interregnum would be worse from the point of view of the fundamental law of nature than a continuance of the existing regime.

The problem we have unearthed in Locke at this point is an interesting illustration of the two fundamentally different forms of argument he uses to justify the conclusions of the *Second Treatise*. One method of argument is deontological and 'deductive' in character. (I do not mean that it aspires to strict deducibility.) Locke postulates the existence of certain natural rights, and makes certain empirical assumptions about the circumstances that would obtain in the state of nature. He then attempts to argue from these premises to how a legitimate state could emerge, to the limits on its powers and to how rebellion could, in certain circumstances, be justifiable. The other method of argument proceeds directly from what would be required by the fundamental law of nature. This method of argument is empirical and consequentialist in character. It says (when applied to the present issue), that any community must be supposed to have a right to rebel, if the consequences of its lacking such a right would be calamitous from the point of view of the values contained in the fundamental law of nature. In the case of a right to revolution, Locke uses both kinds of argument. The argument derived from the original compact, that the majority of the community have the right to revoke the trust it has placed in the political authorities, is deontological and deductive in character. On the other hand, Locke uses the argument that it could not be contrary to the rights of the people to make a revolution if a government threatens their preservation. Here it seems that a direct argument from the fundamental law of nature is brought to the rescue of a somewhat inconclusive attempt at a deductive argument.

Now doubts may be raised about whether it is coherent for Locke to use both kinds of argument. The original ground Locke gives for supposing that persons have natural rights of a certain character is based on the fundamental law of nature. Locke then argues that certain deductions may be made from the postulate that persons have these natural rights, that they enter an original compact and so on. But suppose these deductions were to get out of line with what would follow directly from applying the fundamental law of nature to the situation. One might wonder what independent standing arguments based on natural rights and an original compact would have. The consideration that really counts in the end is whether the prospects for their preservation would be better if the people rebelled than if they did not. The deductive line of argument might be thought to be redundant, or to have only provisional force.

We must now return to Locke's conclusions on when forceful resistance to the state is justifiable. Locke's position would appear to be that if a majority of the community is for the continuance of the trust it has placed in the hands of the government, resistance to the government is not justifiable. And this may seem contrary to our intuitions if the natural rights of a minority are being seriously infringed. Why should they lack the right to resist simply because they happen to be a minority, surrounded by an indifferent majority? Added to this, there seems to be a strong argument as to why they should be considered to have a right to resist, based on Locke's own premises. The only power a government could have is the right to wield the executive power of the law of nature. This, and the power to further the common good, are the only powers that the people have the right to entrust to government. Now the executive power is a power to enforce the law of nature, and nothing else. Therefore, if a minority has its natural rights violated, it cannot be that the government has the power to do this. So why should the minority lack the right to resist? After all, if a member of the abused minority were in the state of nature, she would have the right to resist by force if necessary in order to protect her natural rights. So how could it be that the position of the innocent is worse under the commonwealth than it was in the state of nature? Nevertheless we may continue to be reluctant to allow that anyone may use force to resist the requirements of the state so long as that person is of the sincere opinion that her natural rights are being violated. People can have crazy ideas about what constitutes the violation of their natural rights.

The difficulty we are considering can be mitigated by noting a distinction that has not been made so far. On the one hand, there are acts of individual or group self-defence involving violence against state officials. On the other hand, there are acts of violence against the state in the course of a rebellion. Here there is an attempt to bring down the government, as in the case of the rebellion in Romania in 1989. Locke is considering the latter kind of situation. One can consistently maintain that there are circumstances where it is legitimate for an individual or a minority to use force against the state in order to protect their natural rights, *and* that revolution is justified only if the majority has withdrawn its attitudinal consent. For to protect oneself against the state with force is not necessarily to see oneself as involved in revolutionary activity. One can think that the use of force against the state is justified, and yet that revolution against that state is not.

Therefore the following solution seems plausible. Sometimes forceful resistance to a government is justified in the course of protecting the natural rights of individuals and minorities against serious infringement. In such cases it is not necessary that there should be majority approval before forceful resistance is justified. This is consistent with Locke's view that when it comes to revolution it is appropriate to require majority approval in order for it to be considered justifiable. It would not be appropriate that a minority treated with injustice should be able to dictate to the majority whether the government should be deposed.

The problem we are dealing with is most likely to arise where there are two or more hostile groups (perhaps ethnic, perhaps religious) subject to the same government. If control of the government has fallen into the hands of one of these groups it is likely that there will be abuses of the rights of the other group. Now it may be thought to be an inadequate defence of the rights of the minority to say that it is legitimate for them to resist violations of their rights with force if necessary. For in the circumstances described, this is likely to be a temporary palliative for their position, at best. On the other hand, can a minority be considered to have the right to dictate to the majority what kind of government there should be?

Perhaps a further distinction, alluded to earlier, is necessary to clarify the discussion. It is one between a revolution to change the form of government in a state the jurisdiction of which remains more or less the same (as in the case of the French Revolution of 1789), and a revolution intended to establish an independent state (as in the case of the Easter Uprising in Ireland in 1916). This distinction helps to clarify the situation in several more cases. But it leaves unsolved the problem of two or more hostile communities geographically intermixed, with no possibility of a solution on the basis of separate states. It is scarcely necessary to add that Locke is considering the case where the jurisdiction of the state will remain more or less unchanged after the revolution.

Revolution and democracy

For some time the discussion has concerned the plausibility of Locke's criteria for justifiable rebellion. But even if we were prepared to accept them entirely, there would still be a problem about their application to concrete situations. Resistance to government is justified if a majority of the community has withdrawn its trust. This suggests that there is a *procedure* for deciding whether trust has been withdrawn. But it is not a procedure that already exists within a constitutional framework.

> And thus the community may be said in this respect to be always the supreme power, but not as considered under any form of

government, because this power of the people can never take place till the government be dissolved. (II.149. See also II.168)

How, then, do we know whether Locke's condition for justifiable resistance has been met? Establishing that there is a majority for a proposal in a community the size of the nation-state is a complicated process, even when definitional issues about what will be considered to be a majority have been settled. There must be an administrative apparatus to ensure general conformity to elaborate procedures, and the effective suppression of intimidation and corruption. These are not the conditions we can expect to find in the pre-revolutionary situations where we might wish to apply Locke's criteria. An individual could know that he had the right to resist, on Locke's criteria, only in those cases where it was clear from all informal indications that a majority had withdrawn its consent to the continuance of the trust. It is not denied that the informal indications can be clear enough. Who would doubt that the government of the former German Democratic Republic (East Germany) lacked the approbational consent of a majority of its citizens? The position in Britain in the early 1680s, the situation to which Locke's theory was intended to apply, also seems to have been clear enough on the basis of informal considerations. But the situation would not always be clear in a pre-revolutionary period.

There is a way of remedying this problem, at least in part, if we revise Locke's views on democracy. Locke is a majoritarian democrat when the issue is whether a community continues or revokes its trust to a particular form of government. Locke does not require, however, that the form of government to which power is entrusted should be democratic if it is to be legitimate. This is made clear at II.132.

The majority having, as has been showed, upon men's first uniting into society, the whole power of the community naturally in them, may employ all that power in making laws for the community from time to time . . . and then the form of government is a perfect democracy. Or else may put the power of making laws into the hands of a few select men . . . and then it is an oligarchy. Or else into the hands of one man, and then it is a monarchy . . . And so accordingly of these the community may make compounded and mixed forms of government, as they think good.

Notwithstanding Locke's third option, Locke did not think that power could be entrusted to an *absolute* monarchy (II.90, 91, 92, 93). By an 'absolute' monarchy Locke meant a form of government in which the king is held to be above the law, and can do as he pleases. It is a form of government in which there is no acknowledgement that political power ultimately rests on the consent of the people, and therefore it cannot be consistent with Locke's theory of political legitimacy. Louis XIV was its principal exemplar at the time Locke was writing.

Though Locke thought that political authority ultimately rested on the consent of the majority of the people, he was not a democrat in the modern sense. He did not believe that in order for political authority to be legitimate the main processes of government had to be democratic. Not only does the passage from II.132 clearly indicate this, but his attitudes towards the political events of his day do also. He clearly thought that the administration of William and Mary was legitimate, and personally participated in it as a member of the Board of Trade. But Britain at that time was not, of course, a democracy as we would understand the term. It may be that Locke favoured a radical extension of the franchise, but if so, there is no evidence that he thought that the legitimacy of the British government depended upon this happening. Locke favoured a constitution under which there was a representative assembly, believing this was more likely to further the public good. He also thought that the attempts by Charles II and James II to subvert the place of Parliament were sufficient grounds for rebellion. However, it is unlikely that he thought this because such a representative assembly must be a part of *any* legitimate political system. More likely he thought that the executive was bound to uphold the positive law of the country, and that a representative assembly was a part of the British constitution. We may recall that condition (D) above for justifiable rebellion was that the government fails to respect established positive law.

It can be argued that Locke should not have regarded it as optional whether the community entrusts its power to a democratic constitution. If Locke had said that the constitution had to be democratic he would have had less of a problem with applying his criteria for justifiable rebellion. Suppose successive governments emerge from properly conducted elections under a universal adult franchise. It is true that these elections are not about whether the majority continues to give its attitudinal consent to the established form of government. The elections are processes within that constitutional arrangement for determining who will form the government and who will occupy certain political positions. Nevertheless such democratic processes give an indication of whether Locke's criterion for legitimate government is being met. For suppose candidates opposed to the existing constitutional structure may freely stand for election, but none do, or the ones that do receive little support. Then it is reasonable to infer that the existing constitutional structure enjoys the attitudinal consent of the majority. If a significant number were opposed to the existing form of government they could organize and put up candidates. So when the constitutional form is democratic there is an indirect way of knowing whether that constitution has the attitudinal consent of the majority; a way that is not available when the constitution is not democratic.

Thus it may be argued that the desirability of a democratic constitution – that is, one based on a universal adult franchise, and with the standard political freedoms – is a reasonable implication of Locke's position on justifiable rebellion. However, Locke does not consider this line of thought, and it is not difficult to see why. To advocate a universal adult male franchise was a very radical position for the age, and to my knowledge the idea of votes for women had scarcely been raised in the seventeeth century. Hence this line of thought lay quite outside the parameters of the political culture of the time. Locke presumably thought such a suggestion did not warrant serious consideration. If he had thought of it as an implication of his theory, he probably would have regarded it as an embarrassment. This example shows that caution should be exercised before the implications of a political theory are dismissed as intuitively unacceptable. Perhaps our 'intuitions' represent nothing more than the internalization of some aspect of the political culture of our time.

One or two comments on this argument are called for. Locke apparently means by 'a perfect democracy' a system in which the electorate votes directly on what the law should be. My argument would also apply to the case of representative democracy. Secondly, it would *not* be consistent with Locke's own theory to deny that the community has the right to entrust power to a non-democratic form of government. It is true that if that choice were to be made it would be more difficult to decide whether Locke's criteria for justifiable resistance were being met. The proposed revision of Locke's own position, it must be admitted, restricts the choice of the people on what form of government they should have. Thus there is a sense in which the revised position gives less power to the people than Locke's: they do not have it within their power to choose a non-democratic constitution if they wish. Finally, the argument given for preferring democracy from the point of view of Locke's theory of justifiable rebellion holds only if those *opposed* to the existing constitutional structure are free to advance their views. The point of a democratic constitution, from the point of view we are now considering, would be defeated if 'subversives', in the sense of 'persons peaceably opposed to the existing constitutional structure', were forbidden expression of their view. For then it would be less easy to conclude anything about whether the existing constitutional structure rested on the attitudinal consent of the majority of the people.

Locke's theory of justifiable rebellion would be strengthened if a requirement that the political system should be democratic were added to it. For us, this augments the already considerable plausibility of the theory, as we are disposed to accept the necessity of a democratic system. His theory of justifiable rebellion proves to be consistent with a political culture we are pleased to consider 'more advanced' than that in which he himself operated.

Chapter 4

Property

The correct approach to Locke's chapter on property

Though the property chapter is a very famous part of the *Second Treatise*, it is not easy to understand why it is there. Virtually all of the rest of the book is either about how an obligation to obey a legitimate state can be justified, or about the circumstances in which rebellion becomes permissible. Chapter V, *Of Property*, is not directly concerned with either of these matters.

It might be said in explanation that Locke conceives of a person's natural rights (especially the executive power of the law of nature) as something that a person *owns*, and that Locke also thinks of persons as owning themselves. Might it not be that a defence of property in the usual sense is necessary in order for Locke to underpin this wider conception of property upon

which much of his political theory is based? Unfortunately for this suggestion, however, the property chapter is not concerned with this more inclusive conception of property, but only with a justification of property in the usual sense. The property chapter is apparently very largely detached from the argument of the rest of the book,[1] and it is often discussed more or less in isolation.

Perhaps, though, it is a mistake to assume that the chapter is intended to fit into some larger structure of argument occupying the rest of the book. Perhaps Locke is concerned to put forward a view about economic justice which is not much connected with the issues of legitimacy and justifiable rebellion. In contemporary debate the former of these issues is often raised without much consideration of the latter, as in John Rawls' *A Theory of Justice*. It is true that at present Locke's chapter is usually discussed on the basis of such an assumption. Often, as in the case of Nozick (Nozick 1974, 174–82) it is treated as a resource to be mined for ideas that can be recycled in contemporary debates about the strength of the respective claims of private property rights and economic equality. The right is apt to take the chapter as attempting to show the primacy of private property rights over claims which might be advanced on the basis of economic egalitarianism. The left generally fears a successful defence of private property rights because that might seem to stand in the way of comprehensive economic egalitarianism. (Though it should be remembered that Locke's conception of a private property right is compatible with the existence of welfare claims against the holders of property on behalf of the badly-off (Tully 1980, Chapter 6).)

It would be a mistake, however, to give the impression that Locke's theory is always taken to lend support to the right in matters of economic justice, the left always being opposed to Locke. Some socialists have taken up the idea that labour confers on the labourer a claim of desert in what is produced. This point can then be used as the basis for claiming that the workers are entitled to the whole product of their labour, not just to some of it in the form of wages. Indeed Anton Menger claimed (Menger 1899) that Locke's theory indirectly inspired Marx's theory of exploitation. This strand of interpretation of Locke is, however, almost certainly a departure from Locke's original intentions. Locke proposes that labour provides the title to the initial ownership of something laboured on. But there is no suggestion that in general a person's right to material possessions is proportionate to the amount of labour he or she has expended. This is not to deny that Locke looked upon the idle extravagant rich with some disdain, and that he admired the industrious.

It is unlikely, though, that Locke included the property chapter for such reasons. If he had intended to outline his views on economic justice we might have expected that he would say something about how success in that direction related to the issues of legitimacy and rebellion. But nothing is said on that subject in the *Second Treatise*. Another possibility is that Locke was trying to defend the rights of the property-owning classes against the poor. Now it does appear that Locke did not seriously question the privileged position of the prosperous middle classes. But it would not seem that the successors of the Levellers and the Diggers were a significant threat to the more affluent Whigs in Locke's time. It is doubtful whether there was much serious questioning of the rights of private property at the time Locke wrote the *Second Treatise*.[2]

My own suggestion is that Locke's case for a natural right to individual private property is to be taken as part of a defence of individual private property from threats posed by the *right*, not by the left. We are apt to expect strong defences of individual private property rights to emanate from the right of the political spectrum; from a Margaret Thatcher or a Ronald Reagan. However, this was not the position in the seventeenth century. Charles II wished to raise funds without having to gain the assent of Parliament. The position Locke intended to subvert was that the status of all individual private property was ultimately dependent on the grace of the monarch. (Probably Charles II's position was largely a matter of current expediency, but it also could be seen as a reflection of the earlier, feudal view of property. All possessions are originally held to be in the gift of the King. He then bestows some of these upon his lords, their right to their possessions consisting of their having been given to them by the King. The lords may then, in turn, bestow some of their possessions upon people further down the heirarchy, and so on.) From this it would have followed that there was no invasion of individual rights if the monarch took what he pleased from a subject.

[handwritten margin note: Lockes defense of property against royal property]

> For a man's property is not at all secure, though there be good
> and equitable laws to set the bounds of it, between him and his
> fellow-subjects, if he who commands those subjects, have power
> to take from any private man what part he pleases of his prop-
> erty, and use and dispose of it as he thinks good. (II.138)

Locke, by contrast, claimed that individual persons held their property as a matter of natural right. The existence of this natural right
had priority over any civil authority, and therefore any expropriation
by the monarch was a violation of the individual's natural rights. The
only legitimate claims that could be made against individual private
property rights (except as a part of proper punishment) were taxes that
had been consented to by the representatives (i.e. a majority of the
representatives) of the people in Parliament.

This defence of the property rights of individuals against arbitrary encroachment by the monarch is vulnerable to the assertion that
there is no natural right to individual private property. This might be
said because it is believed that there are no natural rights of any kind.
Or it might be said because it is believed that there is no natural right
to property in particular (though there may be natural rights of other
kinds). Such rights as we have in our property are rights we have in
virtue of the legislation of a sovereign authority. Hence the sovereign
authority always has the right, in principle, to change the arrangements under which particular individuals hold particular possessions.
Of course insistence on the rule of law may be maintained consistently with this position. No arbitrary, unlawful removal of an
individual's possessions may take place.

The view that there is no natural right to private property grants
the sovereign great power over the possessions of the individual (in
the absence of any further consideration, such as that just mentioned).
It allows for any alteration in taxation (consistent with natural justice),
for compulsory purchase, for the commandeering of property in an
emergency or even for the abolition of individual private property altogether. Locke seeks to show that this position is incorrect, and that in
general the sovereign lacks the right to do these things. This is because
individuals may start out with a natural right to private property in
certain possessions, and this forestalls the legitimacy of any such

legislation. Locke is not so much defending the property of the rich against the poor and propertyless; rather he is defending all individual private property against possible unconstrained encroachment by the state. Hence Chapter V is, after all, integrated with the main thesis of the *Second Treatise*: the essentially limited nature of political authority.

There is a further possibility, not considered by Locke, for defending those who have some property against the arbitrary encroachments of the monarch. One might think that property rights were conventional rather than natural, but nevertheless not easily, if at all, alterable. One possibility would be that they should have constitutional rather than ordinary legislative status. Another is that property rights should be regarded as dependent upon the conventions of the society as traditionally handed down, rather than on the conventions of statute law (Waldron 1988, 18).

At this point it will be helpful to note two understandings of the claim that there is a natural right to private property. The first of these understandings would *not* serve the purpose it is claimed Locke had in mind in defending a natural right to private property. The second understanding would serve that purpose.

The *first understanding* of a natural right to private property says that there are good reasons (apart from any reasons that may be supplied simply by something being a requirement of positive law) why we should have a system of private property rights. It also says that there is good reason why every normal adult should be regarded as having the right to be an owner; i.e. no normal adult should be seen as permanently debarred from ever coming to own anything. A case for a natural right to private property on this understanding is comparatively easy to formulate and develop. (It is not necessarily suggested that such a case will be conclusive: the point is that no great difficulties lie in the way of proposing prima facie plausible arguments for this position.) One example is the argument that people on the whole tend to be materially better off under a system of private property rights. An illustration would be the prosperity of the capitalist former West Germany compared to the tattiness of the socialist former East Germany.

The evident difficulty with such arguments for a natural right to private property (from Locke's point of view) is that they are unlikely to establish, unassisted, a case as to why a particular individual should be thought to have a natural right to property in a particular thing. Such an argument, if successful, could, it is true, defeat the view that a government may, with right, abolish the institution of private property altogether. In that sense people may have a natural right to private property; i.e. to there being a system or institution of private property. But it does not follow that any particular individual has a natural right to any specific piece of property.

This brings us to the *second understanding* of the idea of a natural right to private property. This is the idea that, without reference to any system of positive law, an individual could act in such a way as to create a natural right to private property in some particular thing. It is doubtful whether an argument of the kind just mentioned above would establish a natural right to private property in this sense. So Locke tries a different approach. This is the famous 'labour-mixing' argument of II.27. Very roughly, the idea is that when you labour on some unowned thing you mix your labour, something which is part of you, with that thing, and thereby make it yours. This argument, if it were successful, would hold out hope of establishing a natural right to private property in the second understanding. That would make it illegitimate for the state to vary your property right in some *particular thing*, rather than just questioning the legitimacy of the state's action if it were to do away with private property rights altogether. Locke's II.27 'labour-mixing' argument would, if successful, ground the second understanding of a natural right to property which Locke needs. But there is no hope of this argument being successful. So Locke fails to establish the case against the interference of the state in individual private property.

Locke's conception of ownership

Before we consider Locke's arguments for a natural right to private property, something should be said about the concept of ownership Locke is assuming. It is different from that which is usually presupposed in contemporary discussions of libertarianism, and which corresponds to what Becker has called the 'full' or 'liberal' conception of ownership (Becker 1977, 19).[3] The main elements of this conception may be expressed as follows.

If P owns O, then P has the following rights:

1. P has the right to possess and control O, and to exclude others from possession and control of O without P's consent. (*Exclusive control*)
2. P has the right to the benefits which flow from the possession of O, for example, income, enjoyment and use. (*Benefits*)
3. P has the right to consume, waste, modify or destroy O, as P pleases. (*Consumption*)
4. P has the right to alienate O, i.e. to gift, exchange or bequeath O to someone else (say Q), whereupon Q becomes owner of O, provided the exchange, gift or bequest is voluntary. (*Alienation*)

Locke's view of a natural right to property departs from this conception of ownership in a number of respects. Both of the first two elements of ownership are qualified by Locke to take account of the countervailing right of the needy to a share in the surplus of the owners. Regarding the third characteristic, Locke denies that in general owners have any right to waste or destroy what they own, except in the course of consumption necessary for man's preservation and enjoyment. To do otherwise is not permissible in the light of the fundamental law of nature: 'Nothing was made by God for man to spoil or destroy' (II.31). But perhaps the largest qualification Locke makes to the full conception of ownership is to the right of alienation. Owners are not the only people who can legitimately decide to whom ownership of what they own passes. Once civil society is formed the state may re-arrange the distribution of property. But even before civil society is formed the right of alienation is considerably circumscribed in Locke because of his conception of the nature of bequest.

Locke does not think persons always have a right to bequeath property to others just as they choose. The inheritance of property is justified basically by considerations arising from the fundamental law of nature. Children need the goods of their parents for their preservation and comfort (I.89 and I.93). As each child needs them equally for their preservation, the claim of one child on the property of its parents is equal to that of the others (I.91). It would seem, therefore, that it is contrary to the natural obligations of parents for more property to be bequeathed to one child than to another. Hence Locke rejects primogeniture (I.93). Further, Locke says that if there are no 'kindrid' then the possessions of a private man revert to the community: 'and so in politic societies come into the hands of the public magistrate: but in the state of nature become again perfectly common, nobody having a right to inherit them' (I.90). It may seem from this that Locke thinks that a person cannot make a bequest to anyone other than 'kindrid', but in I.87 he seems to indicate that the claim about the reversion of property to common applies only if there are no 'kindrid' *and* if no 'positive grant' has been made to another person. It also seems to be Locke's view that parents may justly bequeath *all* of their possessions equally amongst their children, and that this is so irrespective of the age of the children. It is not clear why this should be just on Locke's own principles, if the children can in any case support themselves, or why it should be just to bequeath any more than is necessary for the sustenance of the children. Even so, Locke has very radical views on the rights of bequest which are not consistent with the views of contemporary libertarians (see I.87–93). It should be added that this interpretation of Locke's views on inheritance is not universally accepted. Notwithstanding the passages I have quoted in support of my position, Simmons (1992, 204) holds that in Locke 'property is individual with free alienation and bequest having priority'.

The 'value-added' argument

Now we take up Locke's arguments for a natural right to private property. We will set aside for the moment Locke's best-known argument in II.27. Instead we will start with the argument to be found in II.34–45. The main idea in this argument is that a system of rights over material things must be such as to encourage useful labour, so that the necessities of life can be created from the natural resources God has provided for us.

But first we must go a little into the background of this argument, and say something about Locke's conception of a law of nature. It has already been said that the denial of a natural right to private property could rest either on a denial that there are any natural rights at all, or on a denial that there are, specifically, natural rights to property (it being granted that there are natural rights of other kinds). So far as I am aware Locke does not seriously consider the possibility that there might not be any natural rights at all. But he does give a general account of how natural rights are justified. From this he can show (though he does not claim that he is showing) that if there are any natural rights at all, there must be natural rights to individual private property.

The general justification of a natural law (and of a natural right) takes the following form according to Locke. We start with the fundamental law of nature as stated in II.183: 'The fundamental law of Nature being that all, as much as may be, should be preserved.' If it is maintained that a particular natural law holds (which in turn confers a certain natural right on certain persons), then the effect of this will be to further the end of the fundamental law of nature. Thus consider the right of the innocent to be free from an attack likely to cause injury or death. If the innocent had no right to be so preserved, this would tend to defeat the end of the fundamental law of nature. Or to give another example from II.16:

> For by the fundamental law of Nature – man being to be preserved, as much as possible – when all cannot be preserved the safety of the innocent is to be preferred. And one may destroy a man who makes war upon him.

In this way it is possible to establish many particular natural laws and their corresponding natural rights, using the fundamental law of nature. Using this method of argument we can establish natural rights to property, for rights of control over material things crucially affect mankind's prospects of preservation.

What natural rights to material things must we have, according to Locke? The background to the answer is that God has placed us in an environment from which we are able to draw our sustenance: the earth, the fruits that grow on it and the animals that live on it. Thus we can discharge our obligation to preserve ourselves under the fundamental law of nature, but only if we are prepared to labour on what God has provided for us. This gives us grounds for saying that everyone has at least one natural right in this area. It is a natural right to make use of the earth and its fruits in such a way as to sustain and preserve one. It would be absurd to suppose that God had placed us in an environment in which we could (i.e. had the physical capacity to) sustain ourselves, and had commanded us to preserve ourselves and yet had denied us the *right* to make use of the earth and its fruits. Now each of us can claim as good a ground under the fundamental law of nature to have such a right as any other. Therefore the basic right of nature in this area is that each person has a right of access to the earth and its fruits for the purpose of preserving herself.

But so far this equal right of all persons in the state of nature is very unspecific. It says nothing about what particular rights particular persons might have to particular parts of the earth and its fruits. How can this right be made more specific? Locke says that God gave the earth to mankind in common. Should this be taken to mean that each person is an equal joint owner of the whole earth? The equal joint owners would then collectively control the whole earth.

Locke rejects this option. For if it were accepted, any particular one of the joint owners would have to obtain the consent of all the rest before she, individually, would have a right of access to the fruits of the earth. Now in the state of nature this consent could not be obtained. So, by the fundamental law of nature, this cannot be supposed to be the situation. It cannot be that no one in the state of nature would have an effective right to make use of the earth and its fruits for the purposes of preservation. As Locke says in II.28,

> And will anyone say he had no right to those acorns or apples he thus appropriated, because he had not the consent of all mankind to make them his? Was it a robbery thus to assume to himself what belonged to all in common? If such a consent as that was necessary, man had starved, notwithstanding the plenty God had given him.

Given we accept the fundamental law of nature this would seem to be a conclusive argument for rejecting the proposal of equal joint ownership.

If this interpretation is rejected, how are we to understand the claim that everyone has an equal right of access to the earth and its fruits? Filmer had argued that if the earth were regarded as given to mankind in common, there was no way in which any individual could come to have legitimate private property (Ryan 1984, 16). Locke's answer begins with the claim that initially no one has an exclusive right to any particular part of the earth. Each person has only a right of *access* (without needing the consent of others) to any part of what is held by mankind in common, for the purpose of carrying on activities intended to provide sustenance, shelter and so on. This assumes that there is not already someone else engaged in that process with which the activities of the newcomer would be in conflict.

Thus it is not enough just to say that everyone has an equal right of access to the earth and its fruits. To be able to make use of the earth for one's sustenance one must have a particular right to control some particular part of it. As Locke says in II.26: 'yet, being given for the use of men, there must of necessity be a means to appropriate them some way or other before they can be of any use, or at all beneficial to any particular man.' But why must there be such a right, even in the state of nature? Why not say that in the state of nature there would be no right, and that what would ensue would be a Hobbesian free-for-all? If there were no right then it would be permissible in the state of nature to (say) snatch a fruit from someone who had already picked it, and who was about to eat it, or to interfere with someone already engaged in productive activity on a desirable piece of land. But if this were how things were, people would give their attention to keeping what they had got rather than to labouring productively. So the supposition that there is no such right is contrary to the fundamental law of nature.

(There is a difficulty here for Locke, the answer to which seems uncertain. Why not say that this unsatisfactory position *vis-à-vis* the fundamental law of nature shows not that there is a natural right to control particular things in the state of nature, but that there is a natural duty to institute civil society? Then there would be a legislative power that could create positive rights for particular individuals to particular things. Locke does not take the view that *all* of the rights necessary for preservation must already exist in the state of nature. The institution of civil society itself is desirable from the point of view of mankind's preservation. But this does not incline Locke to say that there is no need for individuals to consent to becoming subject to a civil society.)

So what should be the basis on which an individual can hold a natural property right over some particular thing? Here the fundamental law of nature comes to the rescue again, in conjunction with certain general facts about the situation in which human beings find themselves. Locke notes that God has provided us with many things which, if we take the pains of hunting, gathering or cultivating them, can provide us with sustenance. But there is little God has provided which will give us sustenance without our labouring on it. So Locke proposes as the basis of the right which individuates the owner of property from non-owners, whether someone has laboured on a thing in such a way as to make it more useful for human life: 'That labour put a distinction between them and common' (II.28). Such a basis for individuation fits with the fundamental law of nature. For those who are engaged in improving things from the point of view of sustaining human life are then protected in their activities by natural right. This basis is the 'natural' one from the point of view of the fundamental law of nature. This is Locke's basic case for a natural right to individual private property.

For this argument to be convincing it must be plausible to claim that a considerable part of the value of that which is improved is due to the labour expended. For we can imagine a situation in which everything that nature provides indeed does have to be modified a little in order to satisfy our needs, but where the change is so slight and easily done (e.g. peeling a banana) that there would not be much inclination to say that the 'labourer' had earned property rights in the thing worked on, especially if that thing available for working on was scarce (Waldron 1988, 192). Locke indeed tries to suggest just such a background for his position in II.37–9. In II.37 Locke claims that appropriate cultivation improves the yield of land as it is found in nature by 10 to 1, or even by 100 to 1. The presupposition of Locke's argument is that goods 'ready for use' are scarce in nature, but that raw materials and land are plentiful. Therefore useful finished goods are potentially plentiful, given that the appropriate labour is applied. Locke puts forward a similar position in II.40 regarding the proportion of the value of things that is due to labour.

It is obvious to us that these assumptions reflect the limitations of the cultures and climatic environments with which Locke was acquainted. Locke is, of course, thinking of cool temperate Northern European environments in which there is relatively slight pressure of population on land (as there was in his time), but where prudence and industry are necessary in order to win a living and to survive through the winter. Had there been a Polynesian theorist of property rights at that time, the same assumptions would not have been made.

Locke takes a severely instrumental view of the reasons why individuals should be able to acquire rights to private property. The knowledge that this right can be obtained makes people more willing to undertake the labour necessary to sustain human life. A 'reward' is necessary because labour is assumed to be intrinsically unpleasant. The creation of things is not expected to be an enjoyable process of self-realization (Ryan 1984, 28). The *virtue* of particular instances of labouring is the improvement of something so as to make it more useful for human life. This is a virtue because the labour is of a certain *type*: a type that will improve things from the point of view of sustaining human life. It is a universal characteristic of that kind of labour. If bread is to be made the grain must be milled, and any distinctive way the miller has of doing this (other than in how it affects the efficiency of milling) is not relevant. By contrast, when we think of people expressing themselves in work it is not, or not only, in virtue of what is universal, but also in virtue of what is particular and typical of that person that we value their labour.

Setting this aside, however, and considering property only from the point of view of how it can be used to sustain human life, Locke's position might be thought to be satisfactory in relation to the fundamental law of nature. But there remain problems in respect of those who are unable to labour productively. Regarding children, Locke says that under the law of nature they have a claim against their parents to provide them with nourishment until they are able to provide for themselves. There are also those who are unable to work because of infirmity or age. According to Locke these have a *right* to what is necessary for their preservation from the surplus of the producers. Locke is very clear about this in the *First Treatise*, section 42, and it is worth quoting at length because Locke is often misunderstood on this point.

The right to charity in Locke (margin annotation, handwritten)

But we know God hath not left one man so to the mercy of another, that he may starve him if he please: God the Lord and Father of all, has given no one of his children such a property, in his peculiar portion of the things of this world, but that he has given his needy brother a right to the surplusage of his goods; so that it cannot justly be denied him, when his pressing wants call for it. And therefore no man could ever have a just power over the life of another, by right of property in land or possessions; since 'twould always be a sin in any man of estate, to let his brother perish for want of affording him relief out of his plenty. As *justice* gives every man a title to the product of his honest industry, and the fair acquisitions of his ancestors descended to him; so *charity* gives every man a title to so much out of another's plenty, as will keep him from extream want, where he has no means to subsist otherwise.

Thus, according to Locke, claims of deserving need give rise to a countervailing *right* against the ownership rights of producers, not merely to a moral claim for charity. It may be noted that this position is re-affirmed by Locke in the *Second Treatise* in sections 5, 6, 70 and 93.

This position is consistent with Locke's overall view. If the fundamental law of nature enjoins mankind's preservation; if there are blameless needy; and if there is enough for all to be sustained, then the needy must have a right against those who already have enough. It is true Locke gives the preservation of the productive labourer priority over the needy, as the right of the needy is only to the *surplus*. But from the point of view of the fundamental law of nature this is reasonable. If not all can be preserved, obviously those who can labour productively should be preserved before those who cannot.

To this claim a qualification must be made. From the point of view of the producers, providing some of their surplus to meet the claims of the needy may be expected to be a disincentive to production. Regarding any increment in what they produce above what is necessary for their own subsistence, the producers may not be able to keep all they have produced. They may lose some proportion of it to the needy. Thus, strictly speaking, Locke's position should be qualified by this rule. If increasing demands on the producers for provision to the needy would actually reduce the extent to which the needs of the needy were met (because of reducing the output of the producers), then demands on the producers should be reduced to the point at which provision for the needs of the needy is maximized. Locke does not appear to consider this point.

The genuineness of Locke's concern for those in need might seem to be compromised by two facts noted by Cranston. One is that in later life as a member of the Board of Trade he proposed very harsh policies for the treatment of beggars. The other is that in her recollections of Locke, Lady Masham said that he hated beggars and would not give to them (Cranston 1957, 426). However, she also said that he was sympathetic to the industrious poor in need, so perhaps his concern was that in the case of beggars we cannot tell whether there is genuine want or not.

Although there is no doubt that Locke believed that the 'full liberal' conception of ownership should be qualified in order to accommodate cases of deserving need, there is also no doubt that Locke was prepared to tolerate considerable economic inequality. It is true that the 'spoilage' proviso on appropriation would appear *de facto* to severely limit an individual's just possessions.

> As much as any one can make use of to any advantage of life before it spoils, so much he may by his labour fix a property in. Whatever is beyond this, is more than his share, and belongs to others. (II.31)

However, this proviso is circumvented if one can exchange that which will spoil for something which will not. With the invention of money, which is a matter of placing an artificial value on things which are not themselves useful for meeting the necessities of life, the proviso is circumvented (II.46–51). For one can nearly always exchange that which will spoil for money, which will not. The use of money may come about before the establishment of civil society. People may 'tacitly consent' to an artificial value being placed on, for example, gold. Without expressly agreeing to adopt this as a currency they may *de facto* create a currency by being prepared in practice to accept gold for goods. Thus Locke is not an economic egalitarian: 'the exceeding of the bounds of his just property not lying in the largeness of his possession, but the perishing of anything uselessly in it' (II.46).

Though Locke's theory is revolutionary with respect to the issue of arbitrary government, it is not intended to imply a revolutionary stance with regard to inequalities of wealth. Locke was seeking the support of the Whig merchants and squirearchy for his revolutionary policies, and therefore he needed to show that political equality in the fundamental constitution of the state did not imply economic equality (Waldron 1988, 148–9).

Many questions can be raised about how conclusive an overall case this is for a natural right to private property. For example, why does the 'reward' for labouring productively have to be a private property right in the thing laboured on? Why not some alternative privilege which would also provide an incentive to labour productively? The rights of control required by the fundamental law of nature would not seem to have to be private property rights. The fundamental law of nature would be satisfied, and people would have 'rights access' to the fruits of the earth, if the earth were regarded as joint property and it was agreed that everyone had equal right of access. It is true that any system of rights compatible with the fundamental law of nature must include the right to consume and destroy things. Ownership rights include this. But a right to consume and destroy can exist in systems of rights other than ownership.

Then why should Locke argue for a natural right to property on the basis of the fundamental law of nature? Private property has a unique characteristic as a system of rights for holding possessions. Because ownership rights permit the present owner of a holding to determine who the subsequent owner will be, the private property system can continuously generate a definitive allocation of rights over particular holdings to particular persons. The question of rights of control over holdings is determined in a 'decentralized' way: the choices of individuals are sufficient (if respected), and there is no call for central authoritative determinations by the state.

Under private property it is always possible in principle to determine which person (if any) has rights of control over any particular holding. By contrast, other systems of rights of control require a central authority to decide that a correct allocation has taken place.

Consider, for example, the principle that rights of control over material things are to be distributed on the basis of need. Under this principle it must be decided by some authority what is to count as need, and what is to be considered as adequately satisfying that need. I do not mean (which is obviously true) that you need an authority to enforce *whatever* system of rights is adopted. Locke of course recognizes that it is better that you have enforcement of private property rights by the state. This is one reason people have for quitting the state of nature and entering civil society. I mean that if you are using the criterion of need for allocation you have to have an authority not only for enforcement, but also for the *determination* of what the rights are in sufficient detail to be practicable.

The fact that a system of ownership rights can in principle operate without recourse to a central authority is crucial for Locke. For if there is any system of rights of control over holdings in the state of nature, it must be operable without the 'consent of all mankind' (II.28). Private property is the only suitable system. Thus it is not necessary that the grounds for some previously unowned thing becoming yours (namely, adding value) should show conclusively that you have established a private property right in that thing. Adding value indeed might equally well be taken to establish some other kind of privilege for the labourer. The point is rather that the privilege in the state of nature *has* to take the form of a private property right. This is the only kind of privilege in this area of human affairs the existence of which is consistent with the assumption that we *are* in the state of nature.

Even if this argument is granted it remains doubtful whether it would establish the conclusion Locke desires: that in civil society people have a natural right to their possessions. For it might be said that on this view private property rights are only a *pro tem* arrangement so that *some* system of rights should be recognized prior to civil society being established. When civil society has been established it then becomes possible to have other systems of rights to holdings. There would be no moral consideration (in terms of respecting people's rights) that stood in the way of making an agreement that there should be a change to one of these.

A further objection to this argument for a natural right to private

private property rights allow mechanism rather than government allocation

property is that the assignment of a private property right as a reward to the labourer might prove to be self-defeating in the long run. Through exchanges, bequests and so on, people might acquire private property rights over extensive possessions. This might allow them to avoid the necessity of labour altogether. Looking at the matter from the point of view of people's deserts, it also might be thought that if labouring on an as yet unowned thing (say land) brings the advantages of ownership to the first labourer, why should subsequent labour only bring the reward of whatever wages have been agreed with the owner of the land worked on? Is it not arbitrary that first labouring should bring such a disproportionate reward (Waldron 1988, 203–5)? But the main thing that is lacking in the 'value-added' argument is that it only establishes a general connection between a system of rights to possessions and the exertion of useful labour. There are many ways in which this connection could be made. It is not plausible to suppose that this argument for private property would much inhibit the re-arrangement of the property rights of individuals by a government. Indeed it might be thought that the partial expropriation of the very wealthy would be in the spirit of this justification of private property, rather than against it.

Perhaps these difficulties led Locke to formulate the II.27 argument, which attempts to make a more explicit connection of right between a particular person and a particular material object. Locke does not clearly distinguish between this argument and the 'value-added' one we have been considering. It seems possible that Locke (unconsciously, no doubt) did not wish to distinguish too clearly between them, and was happy that the impression should be given that the II.27 argument was itself a 'value-added' argument. The actual position is that the II.27 argument, if successful, *would* line up individuals with particular material things. But it is, unfortunately, quite implausible. By contrast, the 'value-added' argument, while providing a prima facie case for incentives to individuals, fails to line up individuals with particular material objects. Thus Locke fails to establish what he needs to be able to show: that it would be a violation of the individual's antecedent natural right for the sovereign to expropriate or alter her property.

The 'labour-mixing' argument

In the II.27 argument Locke starts with the assumption that everyone has ownership rights over himself: 'every man has a property in his own person. This nobody has any right to but himself.' Perhaps Locke supposes that this can just be 'perceived' to be so in virtue of what a person is. Or perhaps Locke regards these rights as derived from the fundamental law of nature in the following way. A normal adult person has a greater natural incentive to take care of herself than anyone else. Therefore if a person has the right to care for herself she is more likely to do it well than anyone else is. As Alan Ryan points out (Ryan 1984, 31) the claim that we have a property in our own person is, on the face of it, in conflict with Locke's view that we are God's property because He has created us (II.6). Perhaps a more accurate way of putting Locke's position would be to say that we have control of our persons on trust, or leave, from God. But as no other *persons* have the right to control us (except with our consent, and then only in particular respects and for a certain time), we might as well be said to own ourselves from the point of view of other human beings. There is also a problem (tangential, though, to our present concerns) about the consistency of Locke's view that persons own themselves with his view that persons do not have the right to take their own lives (II.6).

If persons own themselves then they have the right to control their actions, including the actions involved in labouring. 'The labour of his body, and the work of his hands, we may say, are properly his' (II.27). Therefore a person comes to have ownership rights over what he mixes his labour with, so long as the thing in question was still 'in common' when the 'mixing' started. 'Whatsoever, then, he removes out of the state that nature hath provided and left it in, he hath mixed his labour with, and joined to it something that is his own, and thereby makes it his property' (II.27). It would appear that in this argument Locke is appealing to the following general premise: 'If that which is owned by you is mixed with something still in common, then you acquire ownership rights over that which was in common.' One thinks of the unowned thing as like a colourless liquid to which a drop of blue dye (the labour) is added. The dye eventually suffuses throughout all of the liquid and turns it all blue. If this argument were successful then it would be the person who laboured, and no other, who has the natural right to possess the particular thing. A particular person would be aligned exclusively with a particular possession, and no intermediary of civil law would be required to establish the right of possession.

This aspect of the II.27 argument is evidently unacceptable, for several reasons.

1. Given Locke's general premise, any action which one 'owned', when 'mixed' with something still in common, must result in the acquisition of ownership rights. Now there are various ways in which one could act on things still in common which would not be labouring productively on those things; for example, dancing around them, smashing them up and labouring incompetently so as to not produce anything in the end. But only labouring on something so as to make it more useful for human life gives one a property right in it according to the argument based on the fundamental law of nature. Therefore Locke's position in II.27 is not consistent with the defence of property he offers later in the chapter.

2. Leaving aside the point about consistency, the general premise upon which Locke bases the II.27 argument is in any case absurd. On Locke's view your bodily secretions are part of you (and hence yours in the ownership sense) before they leave your body. But it is absurd to suppose that if they leave your body and mingle with the earth which is still in common, then that which is in common becomes yours. You do not own the sod on which you shed a tear. Closely related to this point is Nozick's argument (Nozick 1974, 175) that if you pour your can of tomato juice into the sea, and it suffuses throughout all the oceans of the world, it would be more reasonable to say that you had foolishly wasted your can of tomato juice than that you now owned all of the world's oceans. Locke does not consider such cases because no sense could be made of them in the light of the argument from the fundamental law of nature. However, such cases do fall under the II.27 argument.

3. But in any case the notion of 'mixing' is unintelligible in this context. We can intelligibly speak of two things of the same kind being mixed up, such as two liquids, or a solid and a liquid. Perhaps we also can say that two arguments have been mixed up. But 'labour' cannot be mixed with the substances things are made of.

To return to the issue of consistency, the main point of the II.27 argument is not compatible with the 'provisos' Locke places upon the initial acquisition of property in the state of nature:

(A)   Before you can be deemed to have started an individual, exclusive right in something that was in common, it must be that 'there is enough and as good left in common for others'. (II.27. See also II.33 and II.34)

The other I have mentioned earlier.

(B)   'As much as anyone can make use of to any advantage of life before it spoils, so much he may by his labour fix a property in.' (II.31)

Now Locke cannot, consistent with the II.27 argument, accept these provisos. For if, when you mix what you own with what is in common, you begin an ownership right in the thing previously in common, then that must happen *irrespective* of whether you have left as much and as good for others, and irrespective of whether what you have mixed your labour with will waste uselessly in your possession. For these external circumstances do not affect the suffusing of that which is yours, your labour, with that with which you mix your labour.[4]

The reasons for these provisos are quite clear, however, if you interpret the assignment of individual property rights from the point of view of the fundamental law of nature. The first proviso is to ensure that the 'rights access' of some to the earth and its fruits does not get 'blocked out' by too many already having appropriated from what is in common. The reason for the second proviso is that if you take more than you can use, someone else's pospects of preservation may be worsened, for the other might have made use of what you have let go to waste. (Strictly, though, it is not clear why you should not take more than you can use if what spoils in your possession would have spoilt in any case. Perhaps Locke's point is that if you do take it into your possession you do not *own* that part of it which will go to waste. Thus someone could legitimately take it from you if she needs it, as it is still in common.) These reasons are the grounds Locke gives for introducing the provisos: 'The same law of nature that does by this means give us property, does also bound that property too' (II.31).

It might also be wondered whether the 'as much and as good' proviso would in fact allow for *any* legitimate appropriation on the basis indicated in the II.27 argument. From Locke's point of view what is available in nature may be divided into two kinds:

1. That which is very plentiful, but which is generally of no use to man as a raw material, for example, sea water.
2. That which is very plentiful, but which is generally of use to man, for example, the fresh water of the Niagara river.

It would seem that proviso (A) applies to cases like (2) rather than (1): in other words, it applies to things generally regarded as 'good' from a human point of view. Locke is suggesting that if, for example, you take a drink from the Niagara river, it would be absurd for me to suggest that you had deprived me of something, as there is still as much and as good for me to drink in that huge river.

It may be allowed that appropriation is permitted in the Niagara case, but in most relevant cases it is doubtful whether as much and as good *is* left after someone has appropriated. Even if the plain extends on and on, and consists of uniformly fertile land (and no one else was there to begin with), land is not as good if it is far from existing settlement. Locke seems to be thinking very literally of the material resources necessary for survival, and not to be considering such things as the disadvantages of being in a remote place. However even from the point of view of physical survival it is usually better to be near the help of settled civilized society. One must also take account of future people when considering the proviso. It may have been that there always was more of the plain to appropriate a long time ago, when appropriation started (again setting aside the claims of any native inhabitants) but there is not now. When considering whether you have left as much and as good, must you consider the position people may be in in the future? If you take this into consideration, then, in a world in which the population is growing rapidly, will there be any significant cases in which the proviso is satisfied? Will it forestall all legitimate appropriation?

Jeremy Waldron (Waldron 1988, 209–28) denies that Locke imposes a proviso linking legitimate appropriation to circumstances in which there is as much and as good in common for others. In Waldron's view the only strict limitation is that what one appropriates should not spoil uselessly in one's possession. This is said to apply to land as well as to produce. One must be able to make use of the land and its products before they spoil. The most important reason Waldron has for rejecting 'enough and as good' as a true proviso is that if it were, it would come into conflict with the fundamental law of nature. If there were not enough land for all to appropriate then the supposed proviso would prevent anyone from appropriating legitimately, and so no one would be able to provide for their needs. But this is contrary to the fundamental law of nature. More people could be sustained if some appropriated and improved the land up to the limit they could make use of, even if this did prevent some others from appropriating. Those unable to provide for their needs by appropriating could either seek employment from those who had appropriated already or, at the worst, seek the charity due to the deserving poor.

It is quite plausible that if the 'enough and as good' condition is interpreted as a proviso it will come into conflict with the fundamental law of nature. It is also plausible that Locke's basic concern, deriving from the fundamental law of nature, is that arrangements concerning property should provide everyone with the opportunity of obtaining a living, preferably through their own productive efforts, as has been argued by Simmons (1992, 293). However there is no doubt that Locke is concerned about the position of the individual who cannot appropriate because others have done so already. Locke expresses this concern in sections 27, 33, 34, 35 and 36 of the *Second Treatise*. It could hardly be said that it does not much bother him. He seems to recognize that there are grounds for complaint if there is no more left to appropriate. That is a reasonable position too, for even if there are other ways in which a person's needs can be met, the person who has not yet appropriated is clearly at a disadvantage in most cases compared to the one who has. In other respects people's rights are equal in the state of nature, according to Locke, but in the economic sphere there would be arbitrary inequalities. (This is not to say, though, that Locke ever thought that his theory of property rights implied that inequality of holdings was, as such, unjust.)

Locke does in fact have a distinct argument for the possibility of individual appropriation from the common stock God has provided.

> He that is nourished by the acorns he picked up under an oak, or the apples he gathered from the trees in the wood, has certainly appropriated them to himself. Nobody can deny but the nourishment is his. I ask then, When did they begin to be his? When he digested? Or when he ate? Or when he boiled? Or when he brought them home? Or when he picked them up? And 'tis plain if the first gathering made them not his, nothing else could. That labour put a distinction between them and common. (II.28)

This argument, however, evidently fails, because when a person has made something hers in the sense of having digested it, she does not necessarily possess it in a way that shows anything about property rights. She would have no right to it if she had stolen what she had eaten. So even if she has digested the apples she has picked, it still may be that she has stolen them, and that they belong to mankind in common.

A yet further and different argument for individual private property rights is found in II.32: 'God, when he gave the world in common to all mankind, commanded man also to labour . . . God and his reason commanded him to subdue the earth, i.e. improve it for the benefit of life.' (See also II.34 and II.35). The labour-mixing argument says no more than that if you choose to work on some as yet unappropriated thing, you can begin a property right in it. The new argument suggests that in doing that you are obeying the command of God, and doing what is rational. Now this consideration may motivate some to labour who would not otherwise have wished to do so. However, if individual private property rights are to be created it is still required that labouring can give rise to property rights, via the process described in the II.27 argument. Simply to carry out God's command to labour does not, of itself, call for individual private property rights. Carrying out God's command *does* require access to raw materials to work on, and therefore it requires access to the earth and its fruits without the consent of all mankind. However, this is consistent with labour normally being co-operative and carried on in groups, and giving rise to communal, not individual, property.

Locke suggests a further argument for a natural right to private property in II.34.

> God gave the world to men in common . . . He gave it to the use of the industrious and rational (and labour was to be his title to it); not to the fancy or covetousness of the quarrelsome and contentious. He that had as good left for his improvement as was already taken up needed not complain, ought not to meddle with what was already improved by another's labour. If he did, 'tis plain he desired the benefit of another's pains, which he had no right to, and not the ground which God had given him in common with others to labour on, and whereof there was as good left as that already possessed, and more than he knew what to do with, or his industry could reach to.

There are, in fact, at least two arguments to be found in this passage. The first is an attempt to impugn the motivation of anyone who objects to a property right being claimed by the labourer. For, Locke suggests, the complainant can begin his own property right in some new thing, given the provisos are satisfied and he is prepared to labour. He is only objecting to the claim that there is a property right because he has a suspect motive: he would like the enjoyment of what another's labour has produced. But Locke's argument obviously begs the question. It *could*, of course, be that the complainant simply would like to have what another has taken the pains to produce. But there is no reason to accept this imputation of an unworthy motive. It *also* could be that the complainant is pointing out that a right to private property has not in fact been established by the labourer. Locke is simply assuming that his view about how a natural right to private property is established is true, and is suggesting that anyone who objects is doing so from a suspect motive.

But there is another way in which this passage could be taken, which is more interesting. Throughout this discussion of property so far it has been assumed that if Locke is to defend a natural right to property, then he must provide us with positive grounds for claiming that such a right exists. But in the passage at present under discussion, we might take Locke as merely trying to show that there is *nothing wrong* with a person who has laboured in the appropriate way making use of what his labour has produced as his private property. To put it in a slightly different way – if someone who has laboured in the appropriate way makes use of what he has produced as if it were his private property, is there any reason why he should not?

It is plausible that a right to do a certain thing can be established on the ground that there is no reason why a person should not act in that way. You have a right to stand on the beach watching the sunset because there is *nothing wrong* with your doing this. However, in those cases where we might argue in this way for a right, the right in question is not an *exclusive* right. The possession of such a right does not particularly advantage its possessor as against anyone else. Anyone has the right to stand on the beach and watch the sunset. But the property rights of a certain individual, if accepted, advantage that person against others generally. Therefore it is doubtful whether the 'no reason why not' approach can be used in the case of property rights.

Property by consent

To date Locke has been interpreted as attempting to establish that there is a natural right to private property in the following sense. Before entering civil society people might very well have private property in particular things. While some variation in the exact terms on which property is held might be made by the positive law of a particular civil society, it is not a proper task of that law to determine initially whether a given object is the property of a given person. The attempt to show this has been said to be the main object of the II.27 argument. This would give Locke the strongest theoretical basis on which to support the practical position he wanted to defend: that the state, and in particular the monarch, did not have the right to vary the property holdings of individuals at will. However, later in the property chapter Locke seems to abandon this position and to adopt a weaker stance. Although the terms on which property can be held may be varied, changes must not be made arbitrarily, but only on the basis of *consent*. I will now trace the path by which Locke arrives at this position.

Locke's case as so far set out assumes that there is sufficient land, etc. in relation to people for the 'as much and as good' proviso to be satisfied. But what position can Locke take when the proviso can no longer be satisfied? If, in due course, nearly all land comes to be owned by somebody, then recognition of individual private property rights will block out subsequent generations from having access to the earth and its fruits, and this will be contrary to the fundamental law of nature. Locke (rather reluctantly) allows that this situation has come about in the settled parts of the world. He insists, though, that there remain (at his time) other places where the proviso is still satisfied, for example, inland North America. (The native inhabitants appear not to be regarded as already having established property rights in the land they occupy.) So how are the demands of the fundamental law of nature to be satisfied in this new, more constricted, environment?

The demands of that law may be satisfied in two ways, given Locke's theory as it has been developed so far.

1. Those who are blocked out from access to the earth and its fruits can hire out their labour to the owners and make their living that way.
2. If they are unable to work, they have a right against any surplus the owners may have to provide for their subsistence.

But a problem with both of these suggestions is that they assume that those 'blocked out' from access to the earth and its fruits are put in that situation without any of their rights (or the rights of others before them) having been violated. But it may be wondered how that situation could have occurred. Some, at least, of the supposed owners must have violated the 'as much and as good' proviso in order to become 'owners'.

Locke's solution is that when civil society has been formed the appropriate property arrangements are to be made by *consent*. These are arrangements either to allow everyone satisfactory access to the earth and its fruits, or else to some satisfactory alternative made possible by the invention of money.

> Thus labour, in the beginning, gave a right of property wherever anyone was pleased to employ it upon what was common, which remained a long while the far greater part, and is yet more than mankind makes use of. Men, at first, for the most part, contented themselves with what unassisted nature offered to their necessities; and though afterwards, in some parts of the world (where the increase of people and stock, with the use of money, had made land scarce, and so of some value), the several communities settled the bounds of their distinct territories, and by laws within themselves regulated the properties of the private men of their society, and so, by compact and agreement, settled the property which labour and industry began. (II.45)

Locke appears to assume that by the time the 'enough and as good' proviso can no longer be satisfied, civil societies will have begun. 'Compact and agreement' are necessary to save Locke's theory when the 'enough and as good' proviso can no longer be satisfied.

Earlier (in Chapter 2, in the section entitled 'The Institution of Government') I distinguished between contractual and attitudinal consent. Both kinds of consent are involved in the present case. In the first instance, the decisions concerning property will be made by the appropriate political institutions of the society. So most immediately, the representatives of the civil society will consent to (i.e. a majority of the representatives will vote for) the proposals on property. But the consent of the representatives can be taken as the consent of the people only so long as the people consent (attitudinally) to the continuance of the trust they have placed in those representatives and institutions. If they *do* consent (attitudinally), then each individual citizen can be taken to have consented. For each individual is said by Locke to have tacitly consented, when entering the original compact, to be bound in these matters by the decision of the majority.

It is usually thought that Locke conceived of a natural right to property in what I earlier called the 'second understanding'. That is to say, particular individuals are supposed to be able to establish property rights to particular things without the need for an existing social convention or positive law. This would make Locke's view of a natural right to property in civil society similar to the view he took of the natural right to self-ownership. You own yourself, and have a natural right to control yourself in the state of nature. You have just the same right to control just the same thing in civil society. The proper role of the state is to protect these rights, and to define them more clearly in certain respects: for example, you have the right not to be assaulted, but what, exactly, is to count as 'an assault'? But it is not within the power of the state to substantially change the nature of these rights.

It is sometimes thought that the same applies in the case of Locke's conception of a natural right to property. If people come into civil society from the state of nature already having property rights in particular things, the state may clarify and enforce the rights of owners, but not substantially re-arrange property rights. This, however, does not seem to be a correct interpretation of Locke in the light of the passage quoted from II.45, nor in the light of the following passage in II.30. 'And amongst those who are counted the civilized part of mankind, who have made and multiplied positive laws to determine property, this original law of nature for the beginning of property in what was before common, still takes place.' It would seem that the state, given that it has the consent of the people, may re-arrange property in a way it may *not* re-arrange an individual's right of self-ownership. 'For in governments the laws regulate the right of property, and the possession of land is determined by positive constitutions' (II.50).

If this is so, what are we to make of Locke's claim that one of the main purposes of civil society is the securing of the property of its citizens? When Locke says that in civil society people have a natural right to their property, I do not think that he can mean that they necessarily have a natural right to retain all the property they may have gained a natural right to in the state of nature. Rather, what Locke means is that property relations in civil society should always be governed by certain *general principles*, even if the detailed arrangements may vary from one civil society to another. These general principles are required by the fundamental law of nature, and are as follows:

The general principles of property arrangement in a civil society

1. Property relations must be arranged so as to provide good incentives for the industrious to labour and produce the things necessary for the sustaining of human life.
2. Property relations must be so arranged as to allow for the able-bodied to make a livelihood out of their own industry.
3. Property relations must be so arranged that those who are unable to support themselves have an appropriate claim against another person or persons who can support them. Thus, those who are needy through no fault of their own have a claim against the surplus of the well-off, and children have a claim to sustenance against their parents until they are able to support themselves.

Provided that these requirements are met, property rights may be re-arranged in positive law in such ways as meet with the citizens' consent. There is no necessity that the rights people had to particular things in the state of nature should be carried over into civil society: those rights are only *pro tem* rights.

Conclusion

Locke's intention in the property chapter is to show that the legitimate power of the state to regulate the rightful possession of holdings is limited. The state cannot, consistent with respect for natural rights, dispense with all forms of private property, for natural law requires that there should be some system of private property rights. Further, persons in the state of nature already may have acquired property rights in particular things under natural law, and if these things are taken into civil society, the citizen's right to them must be respected. Locke however fails to show satisfactorily, even in terms of his own theory, how individuals can have a natural right to property in particular things. Thus he fails in his main endeavour, and in the end has to adopt a partially conventionalized account of an individual's right to property in a particular thing. This allows for a more extensive right of intervention by the state in the regulation of property than Locke would wish. Locke's fall-back position is to allow that the state does have the right to alter the conventions governing the holding of property.

Nevertheless he insists that the exercise of this right must have the consent of the majority. This modified position was still sufficient to protect the propertied against the threats posed by Charles II.

It is appropriate, before concluding the chapter, to give an overall view of the success of Locke's attempt to establish a natural right to private property.

There are certain circumstances in which it is very plausible to say that if a person labours on previously unowned materials, that person begins a natural right to property in the things so produced. For example, suppose an Australian aboriginal artist works on sheets of bark, which are abundantly available. The painting is done with naturally occurring pigments. There is a strong inclination to say that the finished work is rightfully the property of the person who created it, in the absence of any special factor, such as a prior contractual commitment. If someone were to appropriate the work for themselves, or if it were immediately declared the property of a trust for Aboriginal people (without the consent of the artist), we would think that a natural injustice had been done. It is arguable that acceptable conventions governing rights over the control of material things have to conform to our intuitions on these matters, at least in broad outline.

This claim, however, takes us very little way towards establishing a general view about the justifiability of a natural right to property. That is not because our intuitions in the example are suspect, but because the circumstances that have been specified as giving rise to those intuitions are so untypical that they cannot be used to ground a general position on a natural right to property. These untypical circumstances are as follows:

1. Nearly all of the value added to the original raw materials is added by the efforts of one person. By contrast, in nearly all modern production processes the labours of innumerable people are involved, taking into account not only the direct producers, but the makers of the production machinery, the suppliers of raw materials, transport, distribution, etc.
2. The 'production process' in the example given is not capital-intensive. The capital invested does not make a very substantial

contribution to what, and to how quickly, something can be
·produced.
3. In the example given the value of the materials processed is
negligible in relation to the value of what is produced. This is
not typical of most production processes.
4. In the example given it is assumed that the value of the thing
produced is not enormous in relation to the effort expended by
the producer. If a bark painting done in an hour fetches
$ 1,000,000, we do not think that the painter has a natural
right to the whole of that amount. A fairly high rate of taxation
on the proceeds would not conflict with our intuitions about
what are the producer's rights in this case. To believe that there
is a natural right to property does not exclude the idea that
taxation is permissible, especially when the value of what is
produced is very great in relation to the effort required to
produce it.

A better approach to a natural right to property is to start with a
conception of property rights delineated by certain actual social and/or
legal conventions. To say that there is a natural right to property
may then be thought of as making the following claim. There are
principles, supportable by reason, by reference to which actual
conventions can be criticized, and to which actual conventions ought
to conform. Property rights are not to be justified only by reference
to operative social conventions or by reference to the requirements
of political authority. (An example of such a 'rational principle' would
be that rights of control over material things should be arranged so
as to encourage useful production.) When these rational principles
are applied to existing conventions the defender of a natural right
to property will say that it always supports (or nearly always
supports, except for the most unusual circumstances) an over-
whelming case for individual private property rights. They ought to
have a prominent place in virtually any scheme of conventions.
It is in *this* sense that it may be claimed that there is a natural right
to property, not the sense in which individuals are supposed to be able
to establish, without reference to any convention, a property right to
particular things.

Locke is correct in thinking that property rights are not to be arranged wholly on the basis of convention or political authority. It is not for the sovereign power to decide as it wishes. But Locke approached the establishment of a natural right to property from the wrong direction. It was not necessary to show that a person could act in such a way as to establish a property right in some thing without reference to any convention at all. It was only necessary to show that conventions are subject to rational principles, and that the application of these rational principles nearly always implies a very prominent place for individual private property rights.

Chapter 5

Epilogue: Locke's legacy

Locke the conservative revolutionary

It is sometimes thought that there is a cleavage between the radical and the conservative in Locke's temperament. Locke has been presented in this book as a revolutionary figure, but undoubtedly there are conservative elements. The youthful *Two Tracts on Government* (Locke 1967) is conservative and authoritarian. Nor can the existence of both conservative and radical elements be explained entirely by a shift in political allegiance after the start of Locke's association with Shaftesbury. For following the 'Glorious Revolution' Locke became an 'establishment' figure as a member of the Board of Trade. He also adopted a censorious attitude towards the poor in his *Draft of a Representation Containing a Scheme of Methods for the Employment of the Poor* (Locke 1993, 446–61). On the other hand, the *Two Treatises* were

undoubtedly well to the left of the political spectrum when they were published (Ashcraft 1986, 572). The leaders of the 'Glorious Revolution' were not keen to take on board a justification such as Locke's for what they had done, as his position implied that political power ultimately rested in the hands of the people. Not only did Locke defend a radical position intellectually, the course of his life was much affected by his political activity. He may well have been involved in Shaftesbury's revolutionary plotting (Ashcraft 1986, 86–7). He was suspected by the government of subversive activity, and had to spend several years in exile in Holland because of his political convictions.

Defensive and radical revolution

In order to explain these apparent conflicts it is not necessary to suppose that Locke had a split political personality. Locke's temperament remained quite conservative throughout his life. The appearance of division arises if we fail to notice that the adoption of a revolutionary stance can be due to a conservative temperament as well as to a radical one. What I shall call 'defensive revolutionaries' are committed to certain political and social institutions, which they believe to be appropriate and traditional for their society. They believe either that these institutions are under threat, or that they have been swept away by some hostile political power. For example, French resistance to Nazi occupation was a form of defensive revolution. It was part of an attempt to re-establish the former autonomous French institutions in the face of the take-over by an alien political power. Had there been a democratic uprising in Germany against Hitler in favour of the re-establishment of a German liberal republic, this would have been a defensive revolution.

This was the sense in which Locke took himself to be a supporter of revolution. As he saw it, the traditional political structure of English society was under threat from the policies of Charles II and James II. Limited monarchy was threatened by replacement with absolute monarchy, on the model of Louis XIV. This further threatened any independent role for Parliament. English national independence was threatened by French hegemony. English Protestantism was threatened by the re-establishment of Catholicism. In supporting and justifying rebellion against the governments of Charles II and James II, Locke did not think he was seeking to change the political, religious or social institutions of England. On the contrary, he was seeking to *prevent* changes to what he took to be the established character of those institutions. Locke saw the Stuart monarchs as the ones who were seeking to change things and to destroy the established order. This is clearly expressed in II.226:

> this doctrine of a power in the people of providing for their safety anew by a new legislative, when their legislators have acted contrary to their trust by invading their property, is the best fence against rebellion, and the probablest means to hinder it. For rebellion being an opposition, not to persons, but authority, which is founded only in the constitutions and laws of the government, those, whoever they be, who by force break through, and by force justify their violation of them, are truly and properly rebels. For when men, by entering into society and civil government, have excluded force and introduced laws for the preservation of property, peace, and unity amongst themselves, those who set up force again in opposition to the laws do *rebellare*, that is, bring back again the state of war, and are properly rebels; which they who are in power (by the pretence they have to authority, the temptation of force they have in their hands, and the flattery of those about them) being likeliest to do, the properest way to prevent the evil is to show them the danger and injustice of it, who are under the greatest temptation to run into it.

In fact, of course, the 'Glorious Revolution' well may be regarded as something more than a restoration of the status quo. It may have inaugurated additional constitutional constraints on the monarchy, and have extended the power of Parliament. But it was not Locke's intention that substantial constitutional changes should be introduced, or that what he took to be the traditional political structure of the country should be substantially re-made.

Radical revolution

Revolutionary activity is not usually in defence of the status quo, or of what until recently has been the status quo. More commonly it has the intention of bringing down what the revolutionaries regard as an entirely intolerable political (or political and social) structure. The existing structure is perceived to be unjust, corrupt, inefficient, tyrannical or evil. Revolution is thought of in terms of destroying the old status quo and re-making political society in accordance with acceptable principles: justice, liberty, democracy, fraternity, efficiency or equality. The revolutionary cause does not seek a return to the traditional state, but the re-making of society; possibly in a way in which it has never been made before. This was the aim of the French Revolution of 1789, and of the Bolshevik Revolution of 1917. There was something of this spirit in the English Revolution of the 1640s, expressed, for example, in the contributions of the Levellers to the Putney debates. But there was very little of that spirit in the revolution of 1688.

I have just described the stance of the radical revolutionary. Marxism is, of course, a paradigm of a radical revolutionary theory. It is not always easy to say whether a revolution is defensive or radical. Consider the efforts of the Baltic states, Latvia, Lithuania and Estonia, to throw off the Soviet system in the late 1980s. Considering that Soviet power had prevailed since the time of Stalin, we might say that *that* was the established political system. Revolutionary activity in these states was, therefore, radical. But if we think in terms of a longer historical period we might say that these revolutions were defensive: we might say that they sought to re-establish the autonomous non-socialist political systems that existed before the Second World War. It is perhaps rare for revolutionaries, however radical, altogether to eschew defensive rationalizations. Talk along the lines of defending 'ancient liberties' is apt to make its appearance, as it did during the English Civil War.

Locke at home and abroad

Locke's direct legacy to his own country has been a reflection of his character and commitments as a defensive revolutionary. But outside England Locke's ideas have nourished a tradition of radical liberal democratic republicanism. In both the American and the continental European branches of that tradition it has stood for political equality, the rejection of aristocratic privilege, republican political institutions (with a strong tendency towards democracy) and equal liberal rights and liberties, including the guarantee of religious toleration. Often there is some sympathy towards a measure of social and economic equality, though falling far short of egalitarianism. This tradition, nourished by Lockean ideas, produced the paradigms of radical revolutions: the French Revolution of 1789 and the American War of Independence.[1]

But, as so often happens in the history of political ideology, the tradition Locke nourished abroad was somewhat different from the position we actually find in the *Second Treatise*. Locke undoubtedly allowed that republican government could be acceptable on the basis of his fundamental political principles. But those principles did not *require* republicanism. Nor was a republic what he had in mind for the application of his political principles; rather it was the English system of monarchy, House of Lords and House of Commons (II.213). An aristocracy and limited monarchy were quite acceptable. It is true that Locke required toleration and the upholding of what are known to us as the liberal rights and liberties, though for Locke these are not necessarily connected with the presence of republican political institutions. The doctrine of the accountability of political institutions to the people is certainly present in Locke. One might very nearly say that it was invented by Locke. But it is still in a rather embryonic state regarding its institutional articulation when it leaves Locke, compared with how it grew and flourished throughout the eighteenth century in the radical republican tradition.

At the present time those who sympathize with the radical republican tradition find British political institutions wanting in several respects. They are just those respects in which Locke's own views differed from the tradition he has nourished abroad. We may list these respects as follows: a political system only partially and to a limited extent democratic, and defectively accountable; persisting aristocratic sentiments, still of some political significance, together with partially non-republican political institutions; the lack of a fully articulated constitution with a specific formulation of the rights of citizens, and something less than full respect for those rights. The degree to which differences in social and economic class have been institutionalized is also contrary to the spirit of radical republicanism, even granted it never anything like endorsed economic or social egalitarianism. In criticizing the existing situation in these terms we have 'Locke' criticizing Locke: the 'little-Englander' Locke is criticized through the eyes of the 'Locke' who has been abroad too: the universal 'Locke'.

Notes

1 Introduction

1   Locke denied authorship of this pamphlet. See J. W. Gough, 'The Development of Locke's Belief in Toleration', in Horton and Mendus 1991, 76n.

2 Social contract and the state

1   I owe this formulation of Locke's argument to Jo Wolff.

2   For further discussion of these issues see Simmons 1979, Chapter VII, Walker 1988, 1989 and Klosko 1989.

4 Property

1   There is also stylistic evidence that Chapter V was written separately, according to J. R. Milton, in an unpublished paper of his, 'Dating Locke's Second Treatise'. I am grateful to him for allowing me to see this. See also Ashcraft 1986, 251n., 463.

2   Ashcraft suggests (Ashcraft 1986, 251) that the Whigs were
     concerned to defend themselves against the Tory attack that if you
     see people as equal in respect of having equal natural rights, then, in
     consistency, you must seek to level people in respect of property also.

3   Becker in turn follows Honoré. For Honoré's account, see Waldron
     1988, 49ff.

4   I am grateful to G. A. Cohen for this point, who has made it in as
     yet unpublished writings on property.

5 Epilogue: Locke's legacy

1   Laslett, in his introduction to the *Two Treatises* (Locke 1988, 14)
     argues that the degree of influence of Locke's ideas on the American
     revolutionaries has been exaggerated.

Bibliography

Aaron, R. (1971) *John Locke*, Oxford: Oxford University Press.

Abrams, P. (1967) 'Introduction' to Locke, *Two Tracts on Government*, Cambridge: Cambridge University Press.

Andrew, E. (1988) *Shylock's Rights: A Grammar of Lockean Claims*, Toronto: University of Toronto Press.

Ashcraft, R. (1986) *Revolutionary Politics and Locke's 'Two Treatises of Government'*, Princeton: Princeton University Press.

Ashcraft, R. (1987) *Locke's Two Treatises of Government*, London: Unwin Hyman.

Becker, L. (1977) *Property Rights*, London: Routledge.

Beran, H. (1987) *The Consent Theory of Political Obligation*, London: Croom Helm.

Best, Judith A. (1987) 'The Innocent, the Ignorant, and the Rational: The Content of Lockean Consent', in K. L. Deutsch and W. Soffer (eds), *The Crisis of Liberal Democracy*, Albany: State University of New York Press.

Brown, Alan (1986) *Modern Political Philosophy*, Harmondsworth: Penguin.

Brown, Stuart M. (1955) 'Inalienable Rights', *Philosophical Review*, April, 1955.

Cohen, G. A. (1985) 'Marx and Locke on Land and Labour', *Proceedings of the British Academy*, 71.

Cohen, G. A. (1986) 'Self-ownership, World Ownership, and Equality', in F. S. Lucash (ed.), *Justice and Equality Here and Now*, Ithaca: Cornell University Press.

Cohen, J. (1986) 'Structure, Choice, and Legitimacy: Locke's Theory of the State', *Philosophy and Public Affairs*, Fall, 1986.

Colman, J. (1983) *John Locke's Moral Philosophy*, Edinburgh: Edinburgh University Press.

Cox, R. (1960) *Locke on War and Peace*, Oxford: Clarendon Press.

Cranston, M. (1957) *John Locke: A Biography*, London: Longmans Green.

Day, J. (1966) 'Locke on Property', *Philosophical Quarterly*, July, 1966.

Den Hartogh, G. A. (1990) 'Express Consent and Full Membership in Locke', *Political Studies*, March, 1990.

D'Entreves, A. (1951) *Natural Law*, London: Hutchinson University Library.

Drury, S. B. (1982) 'Locke and Nozick on Property', *Political Studies*, March, 1982.

Dunn, J. (1969) *The Political Thought of John Locke*, Cambridge: Cambridge University Press.

Dunn, J. (1984) *Locke*, Oxford: Oxford University Press.

Dunn, J. (1990) *Interpreting Political Responsibility*, Princeton: Princeton University Press.

Filmer, R. (1949) *Patriarcha and other Political Works*, ed. Peter Laslett, Oxford: Basil Blackwell.

Fox Bourne, H. R. (1876) *The Life of John Locke*, London: Henry S. King.

Frankena, W. K. (1955) 'Natural and Inalienable Rights', *Philosophical Review*, April, 1955.

Franklin, J. (1978) *John Locke and the Theory of Sovereignty*, Cambridge: Cambridge University Press.

Gauthier, D. (1986) *Morals by Agreement*, Oxford: Oxford University Press.

Gough, J. W. (1950) *John Locke's Political Philosophy*, Oxford: Clarendon Press.

Grant, R. (1987) *John Locke's Liberalism*, Chicago: University of Chicago Press.

Hart, H. L. A. (1967) 'Are There Any Natural Rights?', in A. Quinton (ed.), *Political Philosophy*, Oxford: Oxford University Press. Originally published in the *Philosophical Review*, April, 1955.

Hobbes, T. (1968) *Leviathan*, ed. C. B. Macpherson, Harmondsworth: Pelican Books. Originally published 1651.

Horton, J. and Mendus, S. (1991) *John Locke 'A Letter Concerning Toleration' in Focus*, London and New York: Routledge.

Hume, D. (1987) 'Of the Original Contract', in Eugene F. Miller (ed.), *Essays, Moral, Political and Literary*, Indianapolis: Liberty Classics.

Jenkins, J. (1967) 'Locke and Natural Rights', *Philosophy*, April, 1967.

Jenkins, J. (1970) 'Political Consent', *Philosophical Quarterly*, January, 1970.

Kendall, W. (1959) *John Locke and the Doctrine of Majority-Rule*, Urbana: University of Illinois Press.

Klosko, G. (1989) 'Political Obligation and Gratitude', *Philosophy and Public Affairs*, Vol. 18, No. 4, Fall, 1989.

Klosko, G. (1992) *The Principle of Fairness and Political Obligation*, Lanham, Md.: Rowman and Littlefield.

Laslett, P. (1988) 'Introduction' to Locke, *Two Treatises of Government*, Cambridge: Cambridge University Press.

Lessnoff, M. (1986) *Social Contract*, Atlantic Highlands: Humanities Press.

Lloyd Thomas, D. (1988) *In Defence of Liberalism*, Oxford: Basil Blackwell.

Locke, J. (1947) *A Letter Concerning Toleration*, in *The Second Treatise of Civil Government* and *Letter Concerning Toleration*, ed. J. Gough, Oxford: Basil Blackwell.

Locke, J. (1954) *Essays on the Law of Nature*, ed. W. von Leyden, Oxford: Clarendon Press.

Locke, J. (1967) *Two Tracts on Government*, ed. Philip Abrams, Cambridge: Cambridge University Press.

Locke, J. (1975) *An Essay Concerning Human Understanding*, ed. P. Nidditch, Oxford: Oxford University Press.

Locke, J. (1988) *Two Treatises of Government*, student edn, ed. Peter Laslett, Cambridge: Cambridge University Press.

Locke, J. (1993) *Political Writings*, ed. David Wootton, Harmondsworth: Penguin Books.

Mabbott, J. (1973) *John Locke*, London: Macmillan.

Macpherson, C. B. (1962) *The Political Theory of Possessive Individualism*, Oxford: Oxford University Press.

Macpherson, C. B. (1973) *Democratic Theory*, Oxford: Oxford University Press.

Martin, C. and Armstrong, D. (1968) *Locke and Berkeley*, Notre Dame: University of Notre Dame Press.

Mendus, S. (1989) *Toleration and the Limits of Liberalism*, Atlantic Highlands: Humanities Press.

Mendus, S. and Edwards, D. (eds) (1987) *On Toleration*, Oxford: Oxford University Press.

Menger, A. (1899) *The Right to the Whole Product of Labour*, London: Macmillan.

Milton, J. (1994) 'Locke at Oxford', in G. A. J. Rogers (ed.), *Locke's Philosophy: Content and Context*, Oxford: Clarendon Press.

Milton, J. (unpublished) 'Dating Locke's Second Treatise'.

Nozick, R. (1974) *Anarchy, State, and Utopia*, New York: Basic Books.

Olivecrona, K. (1974) 'Locke's Theory of Appropriation', *Philosophical Quarterly*, July, 1974.

Parry, Geraint (1978) *John Locke*, London: Allen and Unwin.

Pitkin, H. (1965) 'Obligation and Consent', *American Political Science Review*, LIX, December, 1965, pp. 990–9; and LX, March, 1966, pp. 39–52.

Plamenatz, J. (1968) *Consent, Freedom and Political Obligation*, Oxford: Oxford University Press.

Rawls, J. (1972) *A Theory of Justice*, Oxford: Oxford University Press.

Rawls, J. (1993) *Political Liberalism*, New York: Columbia University Press.

Rorty, R., Schneewind, J. and Skinner, Q. (1984) *Philosophy in History*, Cambridge: Cambridge University Press.

Rousseau, J. J. (1913) *The Social Contract and Discourses*, ed. G. D. H. Cole, London: Dent (Everyman's Library).

Russell, P. (1986) 'Locke on Express and Tacit Consent', *Political Theory*, May, 1986.

Ryan, A. (1968) 'Locke and the Dictatorship of the Bourgeoisie', in Martin, C. and Armstrong, D. (eds), *Locke and Berkeley*, Notre Dame: University of Notre Dame Press.

Ryan, A. (1984) *Property and Political Theory*, Oxford: Basil Blackwell.

Sabine, G. H. (1937) *A History of Political Theory*, New York: Henry Holt.

Seliger, M. (1968) *The Liberal Politics of John Locke*, London: Allen and Unwin.

Shapiro, I. (1986) *The Evolution of Rights in Liberal Theory*, Cambridge:

Cambridge University Press.

Simmons, A. J. (1979) *Moral Principles and Political Obligations*, Princeton: Princeton University Press.

Simmons, A. J. (1983) 'Inalienable Rights and Locke's Treatises', *Philosophy and Public Affairs*, Summer, 1983.

Simmons, A. J. (1991) 'Locke and the Right to Punish', *Philosophy and Public Affairs*, Vol. 20, No. 4, Fall, 1991.

Simmons, A. J. (1992) *The Lockean Theory of Rights*, Princeton: Princeton University Press.

Simmons, A. J. (1993) *On the Edge of Anarchy*, Princeton: Princeton University Press.

Singer, P. (1973) *Democracy and Disobedience*, Oxford: Oxford University Press.

Skinner, Q. (1978) *The Foundations of Modern Political Thought*, 2 vols, Cambridge: Cambridge University Press.

Steiner, H. (1977) 'The Natural Right to the Means of Production', *Philosophical Quarterly*, Vol. 27, 1977.

Strauss, L. (1953) *Natural Right and History*, Chicago: University of Chicago Press.

Tarcov, N. (1981) 'Locke's *Second Treatise* and "The Best Fence Against Rebellion"', *Review of Politics*, April, 1981.

Tuck, R. (1979) *Natural Rights Theories*, Cambridge: Cambridge University Press.

Tully, J. (1980) *A Discourse on Property*, Cambridge: Cambridge University Press.

von Leyden, W. (1981) *Hobbes and Locke*, London: Macmillan.

Waldron J. (1979) 'Enough and as Good Left for Others', *Philosophical Quarterly*, 29.

Waldron J. (1988) *The Right to Private Property*, Oxford: Clarendon Press.

Walker, A. (1988) 'Political Obligation and the Argument from Gratitude', *Philosophy and Public Affairs*, Vol. 17, No. 3, Summer, 1988.

Walker, A. (1989) 'Obligations of Gratitude and Political Obligation', *Philosophy and Public Affairs*, Vol. 18, No. 4, Fall, 1989.

Wolff, R. P. (1970) *In Defense of Anarchism*, New York: Harper and Row.

Yolton, J. W. (ed.) (1969) *John Locke: Problems and Perspectives*, Cambridge: Cambridge University Press.

Yolton, J. W. (1985) *Locke: An Introduction*, Oxford: Basil Blackwell.

Index